Fantastic WATER WORKOUTS

D0483318

MaryBeth Pappas Gaines
Health Education Coordinator
Community Health Plan
Kaiser Permanente Northeast
Williston, VT

Human Kinetics Publishers

Library of Congress Cataloging-in-Publication Data

Gaines, MaryBeth Pappas, 1957-
   Fantastic Water Workouts / MaryBeth Pappas Gaines.
     p.   cm.
   Includes index.
   ISBN 0-87322-458-2
   1. Aquatic exercises. I. Title.
   GV838.53.E94G35   1993
   613.7'16--dc20   92-45783
                                               CIP

ISBN 0-87322-458-2

Lists on p. 133 and p. 135 adapted by permission from *Shaping Up for a Healthy Pregnancy* (pp. 5, 36-40, and 47-55) by Barbara B. Holstein, 1988, Champaign, IL: Human Kinetics. Copyright 1988 by Barbara B. Holstein

List on p. 134 is adapted by permission from The American College of Obstetricians and Gynecologists *Exercise during pregnancy and the post-natal period*. ACOG Home Exercise Programs. Washington, DC, 1985.

Acquisitions Editor: Brian Holding; **Developmental Editor**: Mary E. Fowler; **Assistant Editors**: Sally Howe, Julie Lancaster, and John Wentworth; **Copyeditor**: Nancy Talanian; **Proofreader**: Karin Leszczynski; **Indexer**: Barbara Cohen; **Production Director**: Ernie Noa; **Typesetter**: Angela K. Snyder; **Text Design**: Keith Blomberg; **Text Layout**: Tara Welsch; **Cover Design**: Jack Davis; **Cover Photo**: Wil Zehr; **Illustrations**: Dianna Porter; **Printer**: Versa Press

Human Kinetics books are available at special discounts for bulk purchase. Special editions or book excerpts can also be created to specification. For details, contact the Special Sales Manager at Human Kinetics.

Printed in the United States of America   10 9

Human Kinetics
Web site: www.HumanKinetics.com

United States: Human Kinetics
P.O. Box 5076
Champaign, IL 61825-5076
800-747-4457
e-mail: humank@hkusa.com

Canada: Human Kinetics
475 Devonshire Road, Unit 100
Windsor, ON N8Y 2L5
800-465-7301 (in Canada only)
e-mail: orders@hkcanada.com

Europe: Human Kinetics
107 Bradford Road
Stanningley
Leeds LS28 6AT, United Kingdom
+44 (0)113 255 5665
e-mail: hk@hkeurope.com

Australia: Human Kinetics
57A Price Avenue
Lower Mitcham, South Australia 5062
08 8277 1555
e-mail: liahka@senet.com.au

New Zealand: Human Kinetics
P.O. Box 105-231, Auckland Central
09-523-3462
e-mail: hkp@ihug.co.nz

To my husband, Gary, for his unending encouragement and support; to all the wonderful class participants and clients who have made teaching immensely meaningful; and in loving memory of my grandmother, Marion Chase Jackman, who encouraged me to be inquisitive, inspired my interest in teaching, and helped engender my affinity for aquatic exercise.

Contents

Preface

Water exercise is an excellent way for individuals of all ages and fitness levels to achieve injury-free, effective exercise results. Whatever your fitness goals, water can enhance your success. Water workout techniques make creative use of water's basic physical properties: specific gravity, buoyancy, hydrostatic pressure (which keeps pressure equalized around the joints), and viscosity (resistance). Water workouts apply these techniques to increase strength and flexibility; improve aerobic endurance, body composition, and muscle tone; and enhance coordination, posture, and movement skills.

The aquatic techniques used in water exercise produce overall, total-body fitness that rivals the results of many other forms of exercise. Water exercisers achieve greater involvement of the entire body than is possible during aerobic activities that focus on specific repetitive actions, such as cycling and jogging. Perhaps most important, water motivates you to exercise because it is stimulating and fun. Water makes working out a pleasurable, comfortable, refreshing, and invigorating experience.

In *Fantastic Water Workouts*, step-by-step, illustrated instructions guide you from the simple-to-learn First Water Workout to the well-rounded Basic Water Workout, all the way to the advanced and intensified moves of *aqua power* (push-off moves that build strength and aerobic intensity) and *plyometrics* (jump training techniques that raise aerobic intensity and challenge your muscles). Individuals with special needs will find tailored sequences and instructions to guide them through the Cardiac Recovery Workout, the Pregnancy Workout, the Older Adult Workout, Arthritis Aquatics, and several workouts for chronic-injury recovery, such as the Back and Neck Pain Workout.

This book is in three parts. Part I describes how water exercise can improve your fitness enjoyably and safely. It gives you the information you need to gradually improve your fitness level without the aches, pains, injuries, and frustrations sometimes associated with an exercise program. Part I will get you started with your water workouts by helping you prepare the best environment and equip yourself with a variety of water tools, equipment, and shoes available to enhance your water exercise, or with low-cost equipment alternatives such as common household items.

Part II presents water workouts for flexibility, aerobics, and muscle strengthening and toning, and stresses the importance of warm-up and cool-down exercises. You will find easy-to-follow instructions, illustrations, and objectives for 90 different exercises in this book. Instructions on tailored sequencing will help you devise water exercise routines that are fun, safe, and specific to your objectives.

In Part III you'll learn how to personalize a water workout for your needs. You'll learn about your particular body type and how it affects your workout choices. If you want to use your workouts to help with arthritis relief, cardiac or injury recovery, prenatal fitness, or the physical demands of aging, you'll discover how to set reachable goals and choose the right exercises for your situation. For those who want to intensify their water workouts, a chapter on water power and plyometrics is included.

Water exercise has charged up the fitness world because it provides an effective, comfortable workout that can appeal to almost anyone. Aquatic workouts attract both beginners looking for a safe and comfortable way to get started and experienced exercisers who seek cross-training, new physical challenges, workout variety, or joint protection. When you consider the universal benefits of water exercise, it becomes clear why water aerobics has become so widely popular.

So what are you waiting for? Let's dive in!

Acknowledgments

I owe special thanks to my parents for their tireless efforts in reviewing my manuscript drafts and to Brian Holding of Human Kinetics for his abundant and invaluable guidance. The contributions of Thomas Manfredi, PhD; June Lindle, MA; Julie See; Barbara Holstein, PhD; Sam Feitelberg; Ruth Sova, MS; Jane Katz, EdD; Igor Burdenko, PT; Lesli Bell, PT; John Johansson, DO; Philip Santiago, DC, CCSP; the Aquatic Exercise Association; the Arthritis Foundation; the American College of Obstetricians and Gynecologists; the American College of Sports Medicine; the National Academy of Sports Medicine; and many, many others made this book the powerful tool that it is.

My thanks also go to the following sources for supplying photos. Pages 1, 49, 117, and 176 courtesy of Abraham's Studios, Burlington, VT; page 19 courtesy of Jeff Persons, Manchester, NH; page 40 courtesy of Bioenergetics, Inc., Pelham, AL; page 41 courtesy of (a) Hydro-Fit, Eugene, OR and (b) Charles Razien, Hydro-Tone International, Oklahoma City, OK; and page 42 courtesy of Al Giddings.

PART
I

Getting Fit in the Water

Aqua exercise makes it easy to feel good about fitness. The comfort, effectiveness, and fun of water workouts spring from the extraordinary effect of *hydrodynamics*, the nature of movement in the aquatic environment. Part I provides the information you need to gradually improve your fitness level without the aches, pains, injuries, and frustrations that sometimes accompany exercise. The next few chapters describe how water exercise can enhance your movements and stretches, give you energy and stamina, help you control your weight and improve your body composition, strengthen and tone muscles, increase flexibility, prevent injury, restore pain-free function, build agility and coordination, and control stress.

Water Exercise Benefits

Exercise for fitness becomes more interesting, motivating, and healing when you add the comfort and invigorating dynamics of water. Once you get used to the novel feeling of moving about in the aquatic environment, water exercise gives you a sense of comfort and security you can't get on land. It relieves full weight bearing, prevents injuries caused by falling, takes pressure off the joints, and can help increase circulation. The unique benefits of water exercise have influenced various professional athletes—such as NBA forward Kevin McHale, NFL quarterback Joe Montana, and one-time football and baseball pro Bo Jackson—to use water exercise to speed their recovery from injury and improve their physical conditioning. World-renowned sport injury specialist Igor Burdenko has found that most individuals can tolerate vigorous exercise more successfully in water.

WHY ARE WATER WORKOUTS SO EFFECTIVE?

Water exercise provides an ideal and safe form of working out for just about everyone. By exercising in warm water (80 to 88 degrees Fahrenheit or 27 to 31 degrees centigrade) you can increase the blood supply to your muscles, increase your energy production, increase your body's use of oxygen, and decrease your blood pressure. By reducing stress on muscles, bones, tendons, and ligaments, some people who can't exercise comfortably on land find they can in water. Even people with physical conditions that may limit exercise (such as arthritis, back pain, heart disease, and high blood pressure) can enjoy the benefits of exercising in water. These are some of the main reasons for anyone to take advantage of water exercise:

- Reduce stress on your joints, bones, and muscles.
- Achieve speedy, effective toning through water resistances.
- Increase your exercise work load and burn more calories in less time.
- Stay cool, even when you are exercising hard.
- Experience the ideal combination of fun, effective training, and comfort.

Reducing Joint, Bone, and Muscle Stress

Due to the buoyancy of water, your perceived body weight can be as much as 90% less in water than your actual body weight on land (the percentage varies depending on the water depth). So weight-bearing impact shock is minimal in water, particularly compared to that of land-based running or aerobic dance. With flotation devices, impact can be eliminated completely. Exercise in water is also less apt to lead to the muscle soreness that most people experience when they start or intensify an on-land exercise program.

Impact shock is one of the most common culprits in muscle soreness and joint pain after exercise. Water's buoyancy takes the pressure off the joint capsule, and in combination with the water's warmth, this increases your ability to move comfortably and with increased flexibility. The risk of joint pain is reduced and existing joint pain can be relieved while exercising appropriately in water.

Weight training in water also minimizes the possibility of muscle, bone, and joint injuries because water provides resistance to your body in multiple directions. Let's compare working with a weight on land and in water. On land, muscle tears can occur when you lower a weight because you are resisting the forces of gravity and fighting the weight's downward pressure. In water (because it's more dense than air), as you move the body you meet resistance in both directions because you meet water's viscosity in all directions. This phenomenon also develops balanced muscle strength by working muscles on both sides of a joint during the same exercise.

Toning Through Water Resistance

As an exercise environment, water is more dense than air. Therefore, by harnessing water's resistive power you can speed up your conditioning and enhance your toning results. Pushing or pulling your limbs through water approximates the use of muscle power required for weight training without the discomfort. In fact, with the right water resistance training equipment, water workouts can produce results comparable to those achieved in weight training programs designed to enhance muscle strength and tone.

Because water provides resistance in multiple directions, while gravity (on land) is unidirectional in force, exercising in water lets you accomplish just as much as on land, but in half the time. On land, to work two opposing muscle groups (muscles on two sides of a joint that must be worked evenly to maintain muscle balance, stabilize joints, and prevent injury, such as the front and the back of the thigh, or the chest and the upper back), you must change your position and repeat the exercise. But in water, the resistance allows you to work two opposing muscle groups with each repetition. For example, a biceps curl (bending the elbow to bring the palm upward) on land or in water works the front of the upper arm (biceps). But only in water does the action of returning to a straight arm position work the back of the upper arm (triceps); it does not do so on land. As a result, you can achieve injury-resistant muscle balance more easily, quickly, and efficiently in water.

Other important relationships include the abdominal muscles and the lower back, the hip flexors (used in knee lifts) and the buttocks and hamstrings, the outer and inner thighs, and the shins and calves. To help you balance your muscle work, each exercise, stretch, and movement illustrated in Part II identifies the muscles being worked or stretched. Use this information when planning your balanced water workout.

Increasing Workload and Burning Calories

Because it takes more muscle energy to push your body through water than through air, walking in thigh-deep water or in deep water with an exercise flotation device can give you more than double the work load of walking on land. Your energy utilization system works harder, too. You can burn up to 525 calories per hour of water walking (compared to 240 calories on land) without getting hot and with less risk of injury. For variety and overall improved fitness results, walk forward, backward, and sideways, with short steps, long steps, average steps, step touches, or step kicks. The movement variations and changes of direction can prevent muscle overuse injury and increase your work load.

Staying Cool

A common reason people avoid exercise is that they experience discomfort with increased physical activity. Water workouts solve the comfort problem. Besides reducing impact and joint stress, they won't leave you sweaty. Your body transmits exercise heat to water more easily than to air to keep you cool and comfortable.

Combining Fun, Training, and Comfort

Water invigorates. Splashing around in a swimming pool is playful and makes people smile, perhaps because exercise can be more pleasant in water. Calisthenics become more interesting, more comfortable, and a lot more fun. If you prefer comfort over strain, water's cooling effects and supportive buoyancy make exercises and stretches feel deceptively easy. Yet experienced fitness devotees will appreciate water's high resistance which enhances toning, strength building, and calorie burning.

Your likelihood of success in establishing any new exercise habit rests firmly on the degree of pleasure you get from that activity. Human behavior studies by Ferris and Henderson indicate that, to get someone involved in a particular form of exercise over the long term, "the program must be fun, satisfying, or enjoyable." Those who try water exercise often develop the practice into a rewarding lifetime habit because they enjoy moving in the aquatic environment.

BUILDING A BETTER BODY

"Fitness" consists of several components that affect your body strength, tone, endurance, mobility, and resistance to illness and injury: flexibility, muscular strength and endurance, body composition, and cardiovascular or aerobic endurance. Sport physiologists also identify several motor skills that are considered minor fitness components: speed, power (strength and speed in one explosive action), agility (ability to change body position), coordination (ability to integrate separate motor activities into one smooth motion), reaction time, and balance (ability to maintain equilibrium). Water exercise programs provide many opportunities to move through activities that enhance each major fitness component and a multitude of motor skills.

You will progress in all of the fitness categories when you exercise regularly using the well-rounded Basic Water Workout illustrated in Part II or Your First Water Workout in Part III. The specific kind of training you emphasize will determine which fitness components improve most. Follow a program that emphasizes the conditioning techniques that will help you achieve your personal fitness objectives. The categories that follow provide information to help you choose what to emphasize during your workouts to enhance your health and fitness.

Flexibility

Flexibility is the ability of your joints to move through a full range of motion. Range of motion refers to the degree to which there is movement around a joint. Pain-free posture and healthy, pain-free mobility of the musculoskeletal system require that you maintain an adequate range of motion at all joints. People who avoid stretching or who stretch incorrectly frequently experience joint and muscle injuries that result from inadequate flexibility or joint stress. Range of motion activities, especially in warm water, can be particularly beneficial for people with arthritis, injuries, and joint or back pain.

Muscle Strength and Endurance

Muscle strength is measured by the amount of force you can exert in a single effort through the full range of motion. *Muscle endurance* is your ability to exert a moderate amount of force through a full range of motion over an extended period before the onset of fatigue.

Developing and maintaining good muscle strength throughout your lifetime has been shown to dramatically improve physical independence and mobility in the later years of life. If you want to improve your muscle strength, increase your resistance. To emphasize muscle endurance over strength, lower the amount of resistance and increase the number of repetitions. But avoid high levels of resistance if you have symptoms or risk of illness or injury.

Body Composition

Body composition is the proportion of lean body mass to fatty body mass in your body. Lean body mass includes bone, muscle, tendons, nerves, and ligaments. Aerobic activities can train the body to be a better fat burner, and reducing excess body fat can reduce the risk of heart disease or cancer. However, today people strive—often unsuccessfully—to emulate the unrealistic slender ideal portrayed by movie stars and supermodels. The proliferation of slender role models has helped create an unhealthy, extreme dieting and exercise craze, rampant eating disorders, and exaggerated exercise expectations among both men and women that everyone can and should be slim. Exercise and proper diet can indeed cause an individual to lose weight, but several research studies indicate that it is unrealistic to assume that everyone can develop a thin figure. In fact, thinner is not necessarily healthier for men or women, and studies of mortality rates show similar risk levels for a broad range of body compositions. In other words, keep in mind that people vary widely and that a wide range of body compositions contribute to good health. Weight loss intervention does not significantly decrease health risk unless the initial body fat ratio exceeds 27%.

If you are curious about your own body composition, visit a local health club or sports medicine clinic to have it measured once or twice a year. Remember, there is no completely infallible way to measure body composition, so visit the same person each time and use the same technique to make sure you are making an even comparison from one measurement to the next.

> **Myth: You can whittle down your waistline by performing sit-ups or shrink your thighs with leg lifts.**
>
> *False.* There is no such thing as spot reducing. It's true that you can firm and strengthen soft muscles by performing abdominal exercises and leg lifts. But to lose inches, you must perform aerobic exercise regularly, such as 20 minutes or more of brisk walking three to five times a week. Regular aerobic exercise will burn off stored fat overall.

Cardiovascular/Aerobic Endurance

Aerobic fitness is also called *cardiovascular endurance* because it involves the ability of the heart, lungs, and circulatory system to supply oxygen to the muscles during exercise. Aerobic activity stimulates your body's ability to sustain an activity within the aerobic training zone for an extended period of time. Regular, moderate aerobic exercise enhances stress management, improves sleep, assists weight control, increases fat burning, helps control appetite, improves energy levels, and reduces the incidence of heart disease and other ailments.

BUILDING YOUR HEART, LUNGS, AND CIRCULATORY SYSTEM

There is an optimal level of exercise intensity, called the target zone, required to improve your cardiovascular fitness. If you exercise below the target zone, you will not sufficiently challenge your body to improve aerobic endurance. By exercising above the target zone, you put excessive stress on your system and increase your potential for injury, illness, and exhaustion, without gaining any more fitness.

For an exercise to be aerobic and strengthen the cardiovascular system, it must train the body to do a better job of delivering oxygen to the performing muscles. When you exercise above your target zone, your body must turn to the anaerobic (without oxygen) energy system. This system is designed to work for only short periods of time, which explains why fatigue is the end result of exercise beyond the intensity of your target zone.

A simple way to check your aerobic intensity is to use the "Talk Test." If you can still speak while exercising but are breathing a bit more heavily, you are working at an aerobic level.

Monitoring Your Heart Rate

You can find out whether or not you are exercising at the optimal intensity during an aerobic or cardiovascular activity by monitoring your heart rate. A little practice makes it easier to find your pulse and count the beats. Practice when sitting still and while moving.

One way to monitor your heart rate is to use your radial artery: Locate the pulse with the index and middle fingers of your dominant hand (right if you are right-handed, left if you are left-handed). Gently place your fingers against the thumb side of your wrist (see Figure 1.1a). The thumb is not used because it has a pulse of its own and can be misleading.

A second way to monitor your heart rate is by using the carotid artery: Place the tip of your thumb in the middle of your chin. Move your palm toward your jaw, and place the index and middle fingers at the hollow of your neck just below the jawbone. Keep your head up straight and lightly adjust the position of your fingers until the pulse can be felt (see Figure 1.1b). Caution: Press lightly to avoid cutting off your circulation. If you press too hard you will slow your heartbeat and could become dizzy or faint.

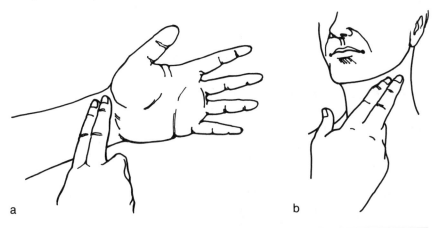

a   b

Figure 1.1 Monitoring heart rate using the radial artery (a) and the carotid artery (b).

Taking Your Resting Heart Rate

Take your resting heart rate after you have been sitting quietly for 15 minutes or, better yet, when you first wake up in the morning, before getting out of bed. Find your pulse at your radial artery at the wrist or at your carotid artery at the neck and count for 15 seconds while watching a clock. Multiply the result by four to get the number of beats per minute.

The resting heart rate count can give you a general idea of your cardiovascular fitness. If your total beats per minute are below 60, you are probably aerobically fit and can maintain your current level of activity. If your count is above 60, you may need to gradually increase your level or frequency of aerobic exercise. There are many exceptions to this rule of thumb, including people who take antihypertensive drugs or have other medical conditions that affect their resting heart rate.

Finding Your Working Heart Rate

Monitor your heart rate during the first part of your aerobic activity and again just after the peak of training intensity. A slow warm-up is important to prepare your body gradually for the vigorous work you are planning to give your cardiovascular system. During this time, your heart rate should build toward the low end of your target range.

To monitor your working heart rate, find your pulse and watch a clock with a digital or sweep second hand. Count the number of heartbeats for 6 seconds and multiply by 10. This will give you your heartbeat rate per minute. Refer to Table 1.1 to determine the beats per minute that correspond to your desired working heart rate.

If your heart rate is below your target rate during aerobic conditioning, take larger steps (within what is both comfortable and controllable), lift your knees higher, use stronger arm movements, or add resistance equipment.

If your heart rate is over your target, move less vigorously, use smaller steps, keep your arms movements small, or reduce resistance.

Measuring Intensity by How You Feel

Personal perceptions of effort are closely related to actual work load, heart rate, oxygen consumption, and even lactic acid (an exercise by-product) and hormones. Therefore, your subjective estimate of work intensity provides an accurate estimate of the level of intensity and the body's internal responses to exercise. Because you are able to judge your effort accurately, it is important to "listen to yourself" during exercise. If the exercise feels too intense, it probably is. The perceived exertion rate scale (Table 1.2) allows you to monitor your exertion easily.

Most people should exercise within the range of "somewhat hard" to "hard" to achieve aerobic fitness. For instance, you will find that

Table 1.1
Target Zone Working Heart Rate Range for Land Exercise

| | Heartbeats per minute | | |
| Age | 60 | 70 | 80 |
	(% of age-predicted maximum heart rate)		
10	125	150	170
15	125	145	165
20	120	140	160
25	115	135	155
30	115	135	150
35	110	130	150
40	110	125	145
45	105	125	140
50	100	120	135
55	100	115	130
60	95	110	130
65	95	110	125
70+	90	105	120

Note: Due to water's effects on the physiology of the cardiovascular system, target heart rates must be modified during water workouts. The Institute for Aerobic Research suggests deducting 15 to 17 beats per minute from your working heart rate when exercising horizontally in water. When standing upright performing vertical water exercise, gravity begins to have a limited effect, so target heart rates from 8 to 10 beats below the land-based rates shown above are recommended.

when you measure your intensity using the heart rate monitoring system, the exercise feels "somewhat hard" when you exercise at a target heart rate of about 70% of your age-predicted maximum heart rate. "Somewhat hard" corresponds to a moderate level of aerobic exertion.

Thereafter, you can use your sense of difficulty to guide your exertion. One of the advantages of using this method is that, should high temperatures cause your heart rate to rise, your perception of exertion will signal you to slow your pace to a more prudent level. The second benefit of using perceived exertion is that it eliminates the need to monitor your heart rate while the challenging environment of lapping water interferes with the ability to find your pulse.

Effects of Water on Heart Rate

Those who exercise both on land and in water often find that their working heart rate is lower in water. Nevertheless, water exercisers

Table 1.2
How Does the Exercise Feel?

Monitor how your heart, lungs, and circulatory system feel during aerobic exercise. Avoid including perceptions of physical difficulty based on whether it is hard or easy to coordinate, maneuver, or maintain your balance or whether the water is making your body more comfortable than on land. These perceptions do not relate to your aerobic intensity.

Perceived exertion rate scale		Target heart rate scale
This perceived exertion value	approximately corresponds to	this target heart rate value.
Very, very light		
Very light		
Fairly light		60%
Somewhat hard		70%
Hard		80%
Very hard		
Very, very hard		

Note: From "Perceived Exertion: A Note on History and Methods" by G.V. Borg, Medical Science Sports **5**(2), pp. 90-93. Copyright 1973 by the American College of Sports Medicine. Adapted by permission.

can gain the same aerobic exercise benefits as they would on land. Researchers at Adelphi University found that even though water based heart rates were 13% lower than land based counts, the water exercisers achieved the same aerobic benefits as their land based counterparts.

This is partly because water assists and improves the blood flow to the heart. Water dissipates heat more effectively than air, and the body compensates by constricting the blood vessels in the limbs. This in turn increases blood flow to the heart (lowering heart rate) and increases the amount of blood output with each heartbeat. Scientists also found that exercise in water results in the same cardiac output (amount of blood discharged by the heart per minute) per liter of oxygen consumed as on land. In other words, even though the heart rate may be lower in water for a similar exercise on land, the body is delivering more oxygenated blood to the working muscles per beat. Therefore, the body is working just as hard to deliver the same amount of oxygen as on land, even though the measured heart rate is about 10 beats lower for vertical exercise, 17 beats lower for horizontal exercise in water.

Preferred Exertion

Preferred exertion is the concept that each of us seems to require a certain level of exertion in a workout to be satisfied. If the exertion is too little or too great, satisfaction is diminished. Training or exercising regularly increases the amount of exertion preferred, and inactivity lowers it.

People who have been involved in competitive sports often prefer a high level of exertion. According to physiologist Brian Sharkey, "(People) have learned (been taught) that exercise has to hurt to be good (it does not); therefore, when they resume activity after a long layoff, they overdo, and end up with severe soreness and injury."

An important word of caution:

Fitness cannot be stored in your body. If you must miss several workouts due to illness or scheduling conflicts, work at a lower level when you return to exercise until you have recovered your original state of fitness.

YOUR BODY IN WATER

Water's unique characteristics make it an excellent medium for multiple exercise goals and for every type of exerciser. The term *hydrodynamics* refers to the physical principles associated with moving your body in water. By understanding how best to utilize those principles, you can devise safe and effective water exercise routines and can more readily perform the specific exercises illustrated in Part II. Several specific hydrodynamic principles explain the different ways that water affects your body. Use these descriptions of hydrodynamics to get started, enhance your water exercise program, and guide your progression.

Buoyancy

The less dense an object, the more it is inclined to float. Humans are less dense than water and therefore are apt to float. Of course, every person has a different propensity to float based on the percentage of fat to bone and lean muscle, and the amount of air the lungs can hold. Therefore, some people experience more exaggerated effects due to buoyancy than others. Greater buoyancy may reduce impact shock, but may also make it more difficult to control movements and posture in water.

The buoyancy water produces can enhance muscle work and decrease the harmful effects of impact shock. The force buoyancy generates can add either assistance or resistance to movements performed under water. Buoyancy makes it easier to move toward the water's surface and harder to move away from the surface.

The water you displace when you enter the water creates buoyancy and produces the nonweight-bearing aspect of exercising in water that makes jumping and running more comfortable. Buoyancy neutralizes gravity and diminishes the harmful stress of impact on the body. Buoyancy and water's equalized pressure around a joint also reduce gravity's pressure on the joint capsule, working with the water's warmth to create a more pain-free environment for increasing range of motion in stiff joints. You will find that you can jump higher, leap farther, run or walk longer, and push harder in water due to the comfortable, protective environment it creates.

Buoyancy can also alter your posture. People who have greater buoyancy, especially originating in the chest and buttocks, may be inclined to arch at the lower back, causing an increased *lordotic curve*. This curve at the base of the spine can put stress on the lower back if the abdominals and buttocks are not held in firmly to maintain a healthy posture. To protect the lower back, and to compensate for the tendency to arch inwardly at the lower back, adopt the pelvic "braced neutral position" described on pages 21 through 22 in chapter 2: Tuck in and tighten your abdominals (the muscles that run over your entire abdomen and rib cage) and squeeze your buttocks together. Remember to breathe deeply while maintaining the abdominal and buttocks tuck.

Resistance and Movement of Force

Pushing against buoyancy creates resistance that can be increased by adding ever-larger or more buoyant floats to the working limb. In addition, water creates balanced resistance in multiple directions because immersion in water exerts hydrostatic pressure equally on all surfaces of the body. Movement in any forward–backward or side-to-side direction meets equal resistance so that opposing muscle groups can be worked equally. A Standing Side Leg Lift, for instance, works the outside of the thigh on the way out and the inside of the thigh on the way in.

Water's density creates resistance that provides the necessary physical conditioning challenge to develop increased endurance and strength. The amount of resistance is determined by the force or speed of your action and the use of water displacement or flotation-oriented resistance equipment. The fitness principle of progressive overload allows you to intensify your results as you become stronger and more proficient: Gradually increase your force and speed or add resistance equipment to intensify your workout until it feels somewhat vigorous without being exhausting. (During each workout, increase only to the point where you can still maintain stable movement control and keep your torso position strong and steady.)

Leverage and Eddy Drag

All movable joints in the body function as levers. You can increase or decrease the work load by using your levers in several ways. For example, you can bend your leg or arm while moving it forward and back and thereby decrease the leverage. You can also change your body position to increase or decrease the body's surface area or to take advantage of turbulent eddy drag (the circular currents created when you move in water).

The flow of water may be either streamlined or turbulent. Turbulence is created when you move an unstreamlined shape through the water. Alternately, streamlined shapes produce a steady, smooth movement of the water.

In other words, during your exercise sequence, straight leg Can-Can Kicks meet with more resistance than the Knee Lift Jog/March (see chapter 3). If you need to reduce intensity, bend the limb that is moving in a forward/backward direction (see Figure 1.2a). During side-to-side movements, however, bending your limbs will increase resistance (see Figure 1.2b). The bent limb intensifies the work load of Floating Side Scissors, Step Wide Side, or Side Arm Pump (see chapters 4 and 5) by increasing the turbulence or eddy drag generated and encountered by the movement of the bent limb.

Figure 1.2   (a) During forward and backward leg movements, reduce intensity by bending your limbs. (b) During side-to-side movements, a bent limb will increase intensity by creating turbulence that elevates resistance.

To increase intensity, present a large, flat frontal surface when moving forward or backward, and your body will work harder against "frontal resistance." For instance, during water walking, put your hands on your hips. The more water you scoop up (the greater the surface area) with cupped hands, webbed gloves, or paddles, the harder you will have to work to move the watery load.

Water Exercise Basics

Befrore you begin, let's look at several key ways to heighten your enjoyment and maximize your fitness success. Learn how to prepare your exercise environment, reduce injury risk, ensure safety, and sequence your exercise routine. Review these guidelines again before beginning your first water workout to ensure your satisfaction.

PREPARING THE BEST ENVIRONMENT

You will get better results and be more comfortable if you examine your exercise environment and determine how you can best suit your needs. Here are some environment and equipment guidelines to help you prepare the best environment for your water workouts.

Controlling Temperature and Humidity

Temperature governs your comfort in water. Warm temperatures (80 to 86 degrees Fahrenheit or 27 to 30 degrees centigrade, 83 to 88 or 28 to 31 if you are arthritic) help increase blood circulation to the muscles, thus preparing them for stretching and reducing chance of injury. When you are not moving and creating heat as a byproduct of energy production, your body may cool quickly in water, so keep moving to stay warm.

Temperatures above 88 degrees Fahrenheit or 21 degrees centigrade do not let the body cool properly during aerobic activity such as water walking or Hydro Jacks; such temperatures are not recommended for a safe aerobic workout. However, nonaerobic range of motion exercises such as stationary stretches, ankle or shoulder rolls, or thumb circles while immersed in temperatures from 94 to 104 degrees Fahrenheit or 34 to 40 degrees centigrade enhance mobility and reduce the joint pain and stiffness associated with arthritis.

When you add the temperature of the water (for example, 87 degrees Fahrenheit) and the percentage of humidity (say, 35%), the end result (122, in this case) must be below 160 to ensure your health and safety. Heat-related injuries and illness could result at heat and humidity sums of 160 and above. A combined temperature/humidity sum of 150 is considered the upper limit for comfortable conditions. If the day is hot and humid, reduce your intensity. If you feel lightheaded or dizzy, leave the water.

Choosing Water Depth

Perform most water workout exercises in chest- to waist-deep water. For more cushioning and buoyancy, seek water at chest depth. People who are overweight and deconditioned, however, may have less control in water that is too deep and might need to begin more slowly or at waist-high depths.

Deep water flotation exercises eliminate impact entirely, providing a totally shock-free environment that allows you to increase intensity without compressing your joints. Water walking and jogging with flotation was first prescribed as a rehabilitation exercise for elite athletes. Each flotation exercise pumps the cardiovascular system by using movements that utilize the large muscle groups (hips, buttocks, thighs) and thereby improve aerobic endurance, burn stored fat, and dissipate the negative effects of stress.

Selecting Appropriate Clothing

A comfortable bathing suit that does not bind, slip, or ride up is preferable for water exercise. Women may prefer the comfort of a bathing suit with straps that cross or connect in back, to prevent their sliding. Shorts and a top (loose fitting but not too billowy) will suffice if you are not using a bathing suit.

If you tend to chill easily, or prefer more support than a bathing suit provides, try wearing a leotard and footless tights along with a T-shirt or long-sleeved top. Aquatic specialty manufacturers such as WaterWear (for addresses, see list on pages 44 through 45) now offer another option: all-in-one water workout gear made of chlorine-resistant lycra, including tights, shorts, and bodysuits with long sleeves and full-length legs (see Figure 2.1).

Figure 2.1   If you tend to chill, chlorine-resistant bodysuits help keep the body warm during water exercise.

Aqua shoes help secure your footing by adding tread to your step and protect the skin on your feet. Several manufacturers offer various types of aqua shoes. Shoes are essential if your pool has a rough or slippery surface or if you need more stability due to sensitive joints.

PROTECTING YOURSELF FROM INJURY

As with any new exercise program, before beginning you should check with your doctor, who will provide an exercise recommendation appropriate for your individual situation. Although most people can benefit from water workouts, readers should be aware of several circumstances in which it is advisable to avoid pool exercise:

- Fever
- Urinary infection

- Open wound
- Infectious disease
- Contagious skin rash
- Extreme fear of water
- Recent heart problems (obtain medical approval and guidance)

Fortunately, most of the conditions mentioned tend to be temporary in nature and present only a passing impediment to beginning a water exercise program. If you are in doubt as to whether or not water exercise is right for you, consult your physician or health professional.

Adapting to a New Exercise Program

Your body will need to adapt gradually to your new water fitness program. Even if you have been exercising regularly, you are introducing your body to a different, new demand, and it must learn to meet the challenge gradually. Gradual introduction is especially essential for people who have been inactive (exercising fewer than two or three times a week during the past several years), injured, or ill. If that is your situation, get your doctor's approval first. Then start out with some simple water walking and static stretching for the first few weeks, and allow your body to develop the basic level of fitness that is required before more strenuous exercise can be attempted without risk of overuse injury or illness. To avoid discouraging and painful setbacks, follow the Initial Conditioning Stage guidelines before you try more vigorous activity.

Initial Conditioning Stage

To develop a basic level of fitness, begin with low-intensity water walking, slowly performed range-of-motion exercises, complete body stretches, and light calisthenics. Starting out slowly and gradually will minimize muscle soreness and exercise discomfort. Monitor your heart rate to be sure you are exercising at the low end of your target heart rate. If you have not previously been exercising at all, exercise lightly for 5 minutes three times a day. When you are ready, follow this initial conditioning program: Using a pattern of exercising every other day, warm up and stretch, then complete 10 to 15 minutes of moderate aerobic exercise such as water walking, followed by cool-down and stretch. You may need from 4 to 10 weeks of initial conditioning before beginning more vigorous exercise.

To prevent injury, always use deliberate, controlled movements, especially while exercising with equipment. Some movements will require that you reduce speed to maintain adequate control of body position and postural alignment. To further decrease chances of impact shock injury resulting from striking your foot, use flotation belts, buoys, vests, and other specially designed equipment during aerobic conditioning. While performing shallow water exercises for aerobic conditioning, begin with smaller movements and increase the range of your movements as you become more fit. Remember, even if you are already fit, increase your intensity gradually over a period of weeks or months to avoid injuries, illness, and chronic fatigue. Overuse problems can result if you don't give your body enough time to become adequately conditioned in response to the newly introduced demands of water exercise.

Injury Prevention Checklist

Of all the information contained in this book, none is more important than the guidelines explained in the Injury Prevention Checklist on the following pages. If you read the guidelines carefully, and go back and reacquaint yourself with them regularly, you will have a much better exercise experience. Before long, these techniques will become automatic, much as the skills needed for driving or riding a bicycle do.

 To protect the structures of the body from injury, maintain the "braced neutral position" (Figure 2.2) during all exercises, stretches, and movements.

1. Stand with your feet shoulder-width apart, legs relatively straight, but with the knees *not* locked.

2. Align your pelvis in the neutral position, not tilted forward or backward.

3. Perform the "tummy tuck": Take a deep breath. As you exhale, contract the muscles of your abdomen. The *abdominus rectus* runs from the breastbone to the pelvis. Think of compressing the long muscles between your breastbone and your pelvis. Tighten the muscles over and under your rib cage by squeezing your rib cage together. You will gradually develop a natural strength that will allow you to automatically keep your abdominal muscles firm and tight during exercise and movement.

4. At the same time, lightly squeeze the muscles of your buttocks together in order to brace your spine in the neutral position.

5. Lift your chest and keep your shoulders back and relaxed (avoid hunching the shoulders).

6. Stand up straight with your torso erect, rib cage lifted.

7. Keep your head level (avoid tilting head back).

8. Breathe deeply and evenly.

The braced neutral position will help you maintain postural stability and prevent injury, particularly to the back. An estimated 80% of the population is vulnerable to chronic back pain. Use of this postural technique can help you avoid a common debilitating and painful health problem.

Figure 2.2   The braced neutral position helps prevent back, hip, and knee pain and represents the foundation for every exercise you will perform.

✔   **Remind yourself frequently to return to the braced neutral position** to protect your back during jumps, leaps, stretches, toning exercises, knee lifts, and many other exercises, particularly those that require you to reach overhead or press your legs back behind you.

✔   **Remember to breathe properly.** It sounds simple, but it is very easy to forget and hold your breath while you concentrate on everything else. Oxygen is an essential ingredient in the energy fueling process. Breathe deeply and evenly at all times to prevent injury-causing fatigue.

✔   **Avoid hyperextending your joints.** Keep knees and elbows slightly bent when you extend (straighten) fully. This "softening" of the joint protects your joints from excessive pressure that can cause tendonitis, bursitis, or other painful injuries. Use this same technique to protect the back and the neck: Avoid overarching the back or neck (hyperextension) during kick backs, jumps, and jumping jacks, and keep your abdominal and buttock muscles tightened firmly.

 Keep your balance. To maintain your balance and protect your musculoskeletal system, move your limbs to complement one another. In the water this means that if you kick your right leg forward, bring your left arm forward. When you press one leg back, bring both arms forward. When you kick your leg out to the right side, bring your arms to the left. Move more slowly and reestablish the neutral position if you find you are losing your balance.

 Bring your heels all the way down. When you land with your feet directly underneath you or in front of your body following a step, jump, or other movement, bring your heels all the way down to touch the pool floor. Repeatedly raising yourself on your toes without lowering your heels can cause painful shinsplint-type injuries and tight, sore calf muscles.

 Monitor your intensity. Take your pulse, use the perceived exertion scale, or check your breathing two or three times during your aerobic phase to see if you need to modify your intensity. To lower intensity, take smaller steps, slow down, streamline your body, or reduce the height of lifts and jumps. To increase intensity, travel more and farther, take larger steps, deeper dips, or higher jumps; alternate between high and low moves; or add resistance equipment. Remember, faster speed is not necessarily a constructive fitness objective in the water. Working beyond your controllable speed or intensity will result in injury and overuse syndromes that will discourage your progress.

• Assess your breathing to monitor your intensity. If you are not breathing a bit harder than you were when you started, you have not yet reached your aerobic target zone. When your breathing rate increases, your "respiration rate" indicates that you have reached the lower limit of your target zone.

• Use the "Talk Test." Can you talk? If during your aerobic exercise phase you can still speak but are breathing a bit heavier than at rest, you are exercising moderately. If you can comfortably speak a few breathy words, you are exercising at the upper limits of your aerobic target zone. If you cannot speak without gasping, you have passed the anaerobic threshold and have exceeded your aerobic target zone limit.

 Keep your muscles warm during the stretch phase. During exercise, the body rids itself of excess heat through sweat evaporation and by transferring heat to the skin where it is radiated into the environment. This process occurs more quickly in water because water dissipates heat four times more quickly and efficiently than air. Gliding movements of the arms during lower body stretches will generate body heat and keep the muscles warm for more effective stretching. Once you have developed torso stability, jog or march in place while stretching upper body muscles. Leave out these peripheral movements if they confuse you, throw off your stability, or if you have sensitive shoulder joints.

☑ **Avoid bouncing stretches during warm-up and cool-down stretch.** Hold the stretch position for 10 seconds during warm-up and 20 to 30 seconds during cool-down to lengthen the muscle safely without invoking the "stretch reflex response," which actually shortens the muscle.

☑ **Increase your workout gradually.** You will save yourself from the pain and aggravation of injury (and even the heartache of the "overuse flu," a chronic cold some people experience when they exercise too much or too often) if you start with a comfortable exercise schedule (for example three times a week for 15 to 30 minutes including warm-up and cool-down) and increase gradually. Give your body a few weeks or so to adapt to the new level of exercise before increasing again. Increase only in very small increments and vary your avenue of increase (frequency, intensity, or duration), or your body will force you to stop altogether. Pain is a signal to stop exercising and seek medical attention or revise your workout.

☑ **Protect the wrist joint.** Keep your hand in a straight line with your forearm at all times. Avoid bending the wrist forward or backward during repetitive movements against resistance (Figure 2.3).

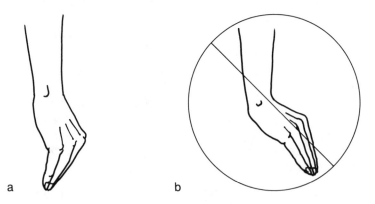

a   b

Figure 2.3 While pushing your hands through water, keep your hands in a straight line with your forearm (a). Do not bend your wrists upward (b).

In addition, when pushing your hands against the pressure of the water, always press with your palms facing the water. Your wrist is more resilient to injury in this position, and you can harness more of the water's resistive qualities. Cup your hand for even greater resistance or use webbed gloves.

✔ **Strengthen your muscles through their full, pain-free, normal range of motion.** Short, choppy, movements that strengthen only through a limited range of motion increase the risk of injury. Keep in mind that overstraightening, also called hyperextension, should be avoided, because it indicates movement beyond the normal range of motion and ultimately leads to injury.

✔ **Exercise your muscles evenly to produce balanced results.** As we learned in chapter 1, opposing muscle groups sustain an important relationship. Injuries result when one muscle is too strong or less flexible in relation to the opposing muscle. Therefore, you must work and stretch your opposing muscle groups equally to avoid injury. People often focus on the muscles in the front of the body and neglect the muscles in the back of the body. For instance, avoid overemphasizing front Knee Lifts Jog/March while overlooking Alternate Leg Press Backs, an exercise that works the lower body muscles to the rear.

✔ **Avoid any movements that involve leaning forward without support and twisting your torso simultaneously.** For example, omit exercises that require you to bring your elbows down toward your opposite raised knee. Such twisting puts debilitating torsion stress on the spine.

Additional Comfort and Safety Tips

1. Protect yourself from the sun. If you exercise outdoors, wear water-resistant sunscreen to prevent sunburn, premature aging of the skin, and melanoma (skin cancer). The FDA recommends SPF 15. Wear 100% UV ray protective sunglasses to protect your eyes from cataracts and other eye ailments.

2. Avoid eating within 1-1/2 to 2 hours prior to exercise, and eat easy-to-digest, low-fat foods. Exercise shunts blood away from your stomach and digestive system and to the working muscles. Sour stomach and food putrefaction can result.

Myth: A quick sugar boost will give you more energy for your workout.
False. A high-sugar snack eaten within an hour of exercise does not enhance your exercise energy and has been shown scientifically to cause weakness and fatigue. Eating sugar

triggers increased production of insulin in the blood. The insulin inhibits the metabolism of fats for energy (which makes eating sugar counterproductive if you are trying to lose fat). It also lowers the amount of sugar in the blood, which may cause you to feel a loss of energy and may reduce the amount of exercise you can complete before fatigue stops you.

3. To prevent chlorine from irritating your skin, shower without soap before getting into the pool. Tap water binds to your skin and helps prevent chlorine from penetrating. Also shower after leaving the pool, soaping all your skin and rinsing well. Soap helps break down the chemical bonds that link chlorine to your skin. Ultra Swim makes soap and shampoo specifically designed to remove chlorine from your body. Finally, use a high-quality light skin lotion after every soap-and-water shower to protect your skin.

4. Never exercise in a pool by yourself. Drowning accidents are unpredictable. Avoid the risk by making sure someone is with you at the pool at all times.

MAXIMIZING RESULTS

The water workout is designed to enhance physical fitness—to elevate physical capacity and improve your overall health and quality of life. To realize the potential gains from your workout, which include cardiovascular endurance, body composition, flexibility, muscular endurance, and muscular strength, your program must be constructed according to a physiologically determined format:

1. Thermal Warm-Up
2. Warm-Up Stretch
3. Aerobic Exercise
4. Muscle Strengthening and Toning
5. Final Cool-Down Stretch

Each time you exercise, begin with a warm-up routine of movements with low to moderate speed and range of motion. The movements help you to tune in to your body and increase blood flow to the muscles. Follow with a mild warm-up stretch sequence to prepare the muscles for more intense exercise and to prevent injury.

Next comes the aerobics section, which improves cardiovascular endurance and body composition. The aerobics component consists of continuously performed large movements that keep the heart rate elevated into the aerobic target zone. Start with a mild aerobic warm-up to let the body adapt to the demand of the cardiovascular exertion and to prevent an adverse response to the shock of sudden high-intensity activity. Gradual cool-down activity at the end of aerobic exercise is essential because it gradually reduces the heart rate and prevents excessive pooling of blood in your arms and legs.

Follow the aerobics section with calisthenics to increase muscular endurance and strength in specific muscles, increase lean muscle tissue mass, and improve body composition.

The water workout sequence ends with a final cool-down consisting of stretching and relaxation exercises to further reduce the heart rate, prevent muscle soreness, increase flexibility, and reestablish your body's equilibrium.

Appropriate technique, body alignment, joint protection, proper warm-up, cool-down, stretch, and gradual progression each contribute significantly to producing injury-free, productive fitness results. The sections that follow explain how to incorporate each of these factors into a full water workout. The Basic Water Workout is a 45- to 60-minute workout designed to exercise every part of the body. It follows the prescribed sequence outlined in Table 2.1.

Table 2.1
Basic Water Workout

Exercise component	Duration
Thermal Warm-Up	3-5 minutes
Warm-Up Stretch to prevent injury	3-5 minutes
Aerobic Exercise—Warm-up, moderate level, peak intensity, moderate, and cool-down	15-30 minutes
Muscle Strengthening and Toning	5-15 minutes
Final Cool-Down Stretches	5-10 minutes

Warming Up

Your program will begin with a thermal, rhythmic warm-up to prepare the body for exercise. Preexercise warm-up generally begins with low to moderate speed movements in the pool to raise the body temperature. You will find illustrations of these movements, such as the Water Walk, Pedal Jog, and Can-Can Kicks, in chapter 3 starting on page 51. The Thermal Warm-Up elevates the body's energy production rate, increases blood flow and oxygen to the working muscles, and improves the responsiveness of the muscles prior to stretching.

The warm-up also enhances the reactions by the nervous system, cardiopulmonary system (heart, lungs, and circulatory system), and the tendons and ligaments. These effects reduce the risk of injury because they improve coordination, delay fatigue, and make your body tissues less susceptible to damage.

Warm-Up Stretch

You will find that stretching warmed muscles feels better than stretching muscles when they are cold and reduces the risk of injury. Hold a steady, static, nonbouncing stretch, and lengthen the muscle only to the point of comfortable resistance. Remember, though, that more is not better. Pain is a signal that the stretch is too severe; loosen up the stretch or review the exercise description and illustration and examine your position to see if it needs to be adjusted. See chapter 3, "Warm-Up," starting on page 51 for the entire sequence of warm-up stretches. Perform every stretch during each workout to ensure overall flexibility.

Exercise Precautions

Injuries will likely result if you stretch beyond your normal range of motion, bounce a stretch, or use a position that puts undue stress on the back or joints. Limit your warm-up stretches to 10 seconds each to avoid overstretching. If you are conditioning for sports, you can prepare your body by rehearsing the sport's movements after stretching statically and before reaching aerobic intensity. During cool-down stretching, work on flexibility by holding stretches longer, about 20 to 30 seconds each. Remember, stretch to the "comfortable point of resistance," breathe deeply, and follow position instructions carefully.

Moving Into Aerobics

The purpose of the aerobics segment is to improve your cardiovascular endurance and train your body to burn fat by challenging the heart, the lungs, and the delivery system that sends oxygen to your working muscles. To achieve this goal, work toward maintaining your heart rate within your target zone continuously or discontinuously for 20 to 60 minutes three to five times per week. Movements that engage the larger muscle groups of the body and that can be maintained in a rhythmic manner over a period of time produce the aerobic conditioning. Swimming, cross-country skiing, walking, hiking, running, and bicycling all qualify as aerobic exercise.

Your body will tell you how hard to work. Use the self-monitoring methods described in "Building Your Heart, Lungs, and Circulatory

System" on pages 8 through 9 in chapter 1 to be sure you are working at an appropriate aerobic intensity. Exercise at an overall moderate rate if you are trying to lose weight or get back in shape. Pursue moderate levels of aerobic exercise to avoid triggering the fatigue that results from engaging your anaerobic sugar burning system and to prevent injury from stress or overuse. Moderate exercise has earned growing support from the exercise science and medical communities. Recent studies have shown that moderate levels of aerobic exercise clearly produce the best results of longevity enhancement and illness prevention.

Progression

Vary the intensity of your aerobics to challenge the body systems gradually and to allow them to cool down gradually. Start with an aerobic warm-up, progress slowly into intermediate movements, then increase gradually to peak intensity, followed by an eased descent into intermediate aerobics, and finish with an aerobic cool-down. Table 2.2 provides a recommended aerobic progression.

Table 2.2
Suggested Aerobic Progression

Aerobic warm-up and intermediate aerobics	Start out with easy continuous movements that work the larger muscles. This gradual increase of activity will allow the cardiovascular and musculoskeletal systems to adjust gradually to increasing exercise demands. Keep movements smaller and slower in the beginning, then gradually quicken the pace, use larger movements, and cover more territory while moving about the pool.
Peak aerobics	Now that you have gradually built your intensity, continue exercising at this elevated heart rate. Use large, controlled movements, change direction, travel around the pool, vary high and low steps, use jumps and flutter kicks, and maintain a high intensity within your working range.
Intermediate aerobics and aerobic cool-down	Many people forget to cool down gradually by progressively changing to smaller movements, reducing travel about the pool, and

(continued)

Table 2.2   (continued)

Intermediate aerobics and aerobic cool-down	lessening impact by eliminating jumping motions. The aerobic cool-down allows the body to gradually readjust to lower intensity, lessening the risk of damage to the cardiovascular system. Cardiac complications occur most often when exercise ceases abruptly, so continue to gradually lower the heart rate to 120 beats per minute, or the low end of your target zone, whichever is lower. Gradual cool-down helps prevent excessive pooling of blood in the extremities, prevents dizziness, and reduces muscle soreness. Avoid calf soreness by bringing the heels all the way down to the floor on each landing whenever body position allows. Drinking enough water also helps prevent muscle cramping.

Exercise Precautions

Balance the amount of exercise for the various muscle groups by using movements to the front, back, and sides and on various diagonals. Exercisers often forget to work the muscles on the sides and back of the body. Remind yourself often to press back, kick side, and "kick up your heels" (back leg curls). Figure 2.4 illustrates examples of front, side, and back movements for overall conditioning balance. Vary stresses on the joints by alternating movements frequently, such as every 8 or 16 counts. The objective during the aerobic section is to choose exercises that challenge different muscle groups rather than reusing the same muscle group in the same way over and over. Focus on maintaining the braced neutral position during all aerobic exercise, particularly when jumping, landing, or raising the arms.

Calisthenics for Strengthening and Toning

Toning serves as the major objective for many exercisers. However, muscle strengthening through calisthenics can also enhance resilience to injury, increase muscle endurance, and aid in weight control by improving the lean-to-fat tissue ratio. (Remember, fat cannot become muscle, nor can muscle become fat. Fat must be burned aerobically, and muscle tissue must be developed by performing strengthening and endurance exercises.)

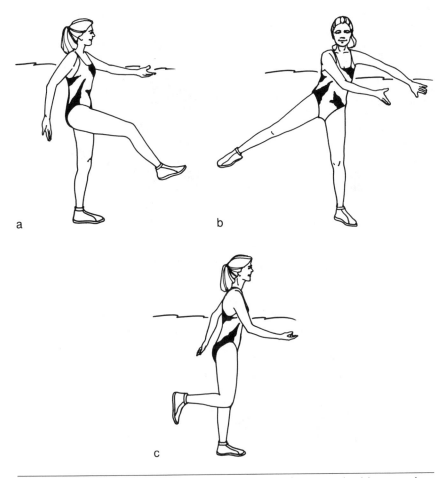

Figure 2.4   Balance your workout by working your front muscles (a), your side muscles (b), and your rear muscles (c).

If you need to protect a previously injured or sensitive area, do more repetitions at lower resistance to encourage pain-free benefits. To build maximum strength, use higher resistance and fewer repetitions. Add resistance by employing your own body weight or by using resistance equipment. You must coordinate flexibility training, gradual progression, and appropriate warm-up with strength training to ensure adequate injury prevention.

Strengthening and Toning Hips and Thighs

Familiarize yourself with the anatomy of the lower body (Figure 2.5). While improvements in appearance aid in motivation, the real objective

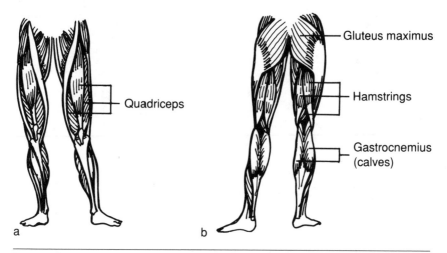

Figure 2.5   The muscles of the lower body from the front (a) and back (b).

here is knee and hip strength. Remember, aerobic exercise will reduce the fat storage in your body. Healthy appearance and attractive posture come along with conditioned, balanced muscles. Strengthen the thighs, front, back, and sides using front leg kicks, back knee curls, and side lunge steps, to protect the knee and hip. Strengthen the hip with knee lifts, press backs, and side leg lifts. Do water squats to strengthen the buttocks and thighs, and include them in movement combinations to work the entire lower body effectively. See Chapter 5 for specifics on exercises to strengthen and tone the lower body.

Exercise Precautions

To ensure back safety, the pelvis must be braced in the neutral position and the abdominal and buttocks muscles contracted throughout each exercise. Avoid hyperextending the lower back by jutting out the stomach and curving the lower back. Move at a speed that allows you to perform each exercise in complete control, without losing your positioning.

Firming Abdominal Muscles

Abdominal exercise represents one of the most universally beneficial fitness activities you can pursue. While abdominal exercise can't give you a trimmer waistline (only regular aerobic exercise and an energy-balanced, nutritious, low-fat diet can do that), it is essential for good posture, low back injury prevention, and adequate support for the stomach and intestines. The abdominal muscle group (Figure 2.6) flexes, rotates, and contracts the trunk. Strong abdominals contribute to trunk

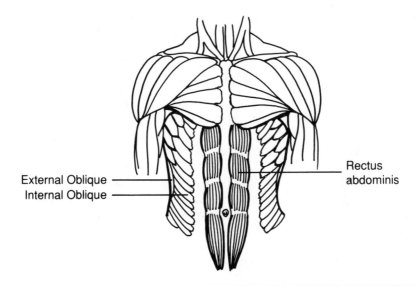

External Oblique
Internal Oblique

Rectus
abdominis

Figure 2.6   The muscles of the abdomen include the rectus abdominis and the internal and external obliques.

and pelvic stability, elements crucial to long-term injury prevention and physical independence in middle and later life.

Abdominal muscles are slow to condition unless exposed to repeated resistance and varied challenge. In water you can more easily develop body and breathing awareness, reduce chance of injury due to improper technique or overzealousness, and use strength-building resistance.

Exercise Precautions

Avoid exercises that force the back into unprotected hyperextension (backward arch) during movement, or exercises that require holding water jugs or other flotation devices at arm's length (strains the back, the shoulder, the neck, and the elbow joints). When using jugs, hold them firmly under the arm with open palms around the jug handles. Grasping the handles too firmly can elevate the blood pressure or aggravate arthritis in the hands. Those who are not comfortable with jugs (people with shoulder injuries, arthritis, bursitis, or hand limitations) should use alternate flotation such as Sprint flotation belts, Body Buoys, the Wet Vest, Free Floater upper arm rings, or other appropriate flotation devices that do not force the user into a forward or backward position.

Remember that when the abdominal muscles become fatigued, they cannot protect the spine from painful hyperextension. Slow, continuous exercises ceased before fatigue sets in will protect you from developing low back injury brought on by overenthusiastic abdominal exercise. Many people will find that, in the water, they can perform more exercises with better control, maintain more comfortable body position, and gain more strength with reduced risk of injury.

Using Water to Your Advantage

Water is the perfect environment for abdominal exercise because it can protect the back from injury during the quest for sleek and strong abdominal muscles. In the water, buoyancy permits defiance of gravity, the main culprit in the onset of back pain. (Humans were originally designed to walk on all fours; somewhere in the evolutionary process we thumbed our noses at the forces of gravity, but our spinal anatomy remains inadequately adapted to meet the rigors of upright locomotion.) Buoyancy takes stress off the joints involved in almost any movement performed in the water, including abdominal exercises.

Many people find land-based abdominal exercises difficult and ineffective. Control is awkward for the novice, and even some experienced exercisers expose themselves to injury by jerking their necks forward or arching their backs while straining to achieve results. Water workout abdominal exercises enable you to use water's resistance in the protective environment of aquatic buoyancy. With the right techniques, you can build strength by working the abodminal muscles both alone and in coordination with the back and hips. Learn about muscle control, positioning, and breathing by performing the abdominal exercises described in chapter 5.

Back Extensions

In addition to abdominal muscle strengthening and back/lower body flexibility conditioning, physicians recommend maintaining strong back extensor muscles to ward off lower back pain caused by muscle weakness. To gently strengthen these muscles while standing in the pool, begin in a flat back position (Figure 2.7a), place your hands at mid thigh, and round your back toward the sky to form a "mountain" shape (Figure 2.7b). Then return to a flat back position, continually supporting your weight with your hands on your thighs. For improved back flexibility and strength, repeat the exercise illustrated in Figure 2.7 slowly several times and finish with a 20-second static stretch in the position shown in Figure 2.7b.

Strengthening Your Upper Body

Balanced strength in the upper torso muscles (Figure 2.8) can help prevent or correct postural problems such as rounded shoulders. Water exercise balances and strengthens the shoulders, chest, and upper back by working the body against resistance in both directions during the

Figure 2.7   Back extensions: Begin in the flat position (a) and round your back into a "mountain" shape (b).

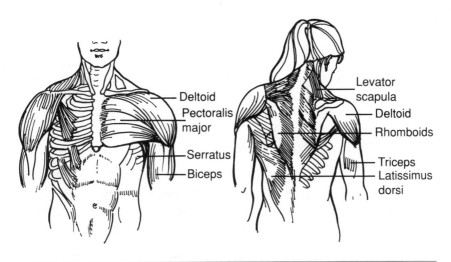

Figure 2.8   The muscles of the upper body from the front (a) and back (b).

same exercise. The complete exercise program illustrated in chapter 5 provides a sequence that conditions the upper body muscles for the purpose of developing healthy, balanced musculature.

Start without disks or resistance, then gradually increase the degree of intensity by adding resistance equipment, starting at slower speeds and building as you become stronger.

Exercise Precautions

Maintain a stable position with your feet planted firmly on the bottom of the pool and your body aligned in the neutral position (Figure 2.9a).

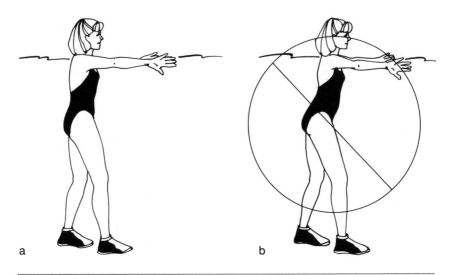

a   b

Figure 2.9   Begin in the braced neutral position with one leg forward and one leg back (a). Avoid lumbar spine hyperextension (b).

The muscles of the torso work as stabilizers during upper body exercises. As you become stronger, you can march in place to stay warm. Avoid hyperextending the lower back (Figure 2.9b).

Strengthening Your Shins

Walk on your heels or tap your toes to work the front of the lower leg. Most of the shallow water aerobic exercises you perform work the calf, so you will need to strengthen the shins to keep the muscles in balance and prevent injury.

Cooling Down and Increasing Flexibility

Warm muscles respond well to flexibility exercises. The stretches performed at the end of your exercise routine are designed to maintain or increase flexibility around the body joints. During the final stretch, maintain static, steady stretch positions for 10 to 30 seconds each to let the muscle completely relax and cool in its fully lengthened position. Adequate flexibility is the key for preventing injury. However, once again, more is not better. Stretching should never hurt.

Exercise Precautions

Hold the position and stretch to the point where you feel comfortable resistance but no pain. Bouncing a stretch will produce microscopic tears in the muscle and can actually cause the muscle to shorten. Follow the stretch instructions carefully to be sure you are in the proper position, with all joints protected. Everyone exhibits differing degrees of flexibility, so avoid comparing yourself to someone else. Do what feels comfortable for you. You may find that you feel more flexible on some days than others, so listen to your body and adjust the degree of stretch according to how you feel that day.

PROGRESSING INTO TRANSITIONS

Change gradually from one movement to the next to give your body a chance to adjust safely. Smooth transitions will cut your risk of injury. Gliding easily from movement to movement takes practice, but it's worth the effort and comes naturally after a short time. You will find it easier to make transitions if you use a simple move between two complex actions. In other words, alternate between simple exercises (Pedal Jog, Hydro Jacks, Knee Lift Jog/March, Kick Up Your Heels) and more complex movements (Step Wide Side, Rocking Horse, Cross-Country Ski). See chapters 3 and 4 for exercise diagrams.

Some transitions are called progressions because you add to the exercise by changing only one aspect of your movement at a time. For example, begin a movement of the legs without upper body movement. Then add a movement of your arms without changing the movement of the legs. Next, change the direction or height of the exercise.

The key is to avoid changing too many aspects at once. You will find that adding changes one by one will be more comfortable and will enable you to exercise smoothly and continuously. The various types of changes made during transitions include

- upper body action changes;
- lower body action changes;
- stationary activity vs. traveling moves from place to place;
- directional changes (turn or travel left, right, front, back);
- forward/backward moves vs. lateral moves (side to side);
- movement height changes (high, low, medium);
- change to flotation; and
- vertical vs. horizontal flotation.

You can pyramid your changes by building a simple action step-by-step into a more complex movement. Add new transitions one by one to your original, simple move to build a pyramid. Or continuously change various aspects of your movements to progress through a variety of motions. Variety will keep you motivated, work your muscles in balance, and keep you from overworking one muscle group while neglecting another.

THE IMPORTANCE OF DRINKING WATER

Although you don't feel it as much as in land-based exercise, you do perspire during water workouts. Your body can become dehydrated during water exercise, and replenishing fluids regularly is vital for your safety.

To prevent fatigue, it is essential to keep your body hydrated before, during, and after water exercise, particularly in hot or humid environments. The best way to replace lost fluids is by drinking plain water rather than soda, juice, or coffee. These alternatives can actually contribute to dehydration. Always keep a plastic container filled with drinking water near the pool edge.

> **Myth: You shouldn't drink water when you exercise, because it will give you cramps and make you nauseated.**
>
> *False.* Strive to drink eight 8-ounce or 240 ml glasses of water a day, plus two an hour before exercise and two glasses after. You can drink more during exercise, especially if your activity is of long duration. Drink greater amounts of water in hot, cold, or humid weather. (Hot or humid weather makes you lose more fluids through sweat; cold weather activates the kidneys, stimulating increased urination.) Each can cause you to become dehydrated more easily. In some cases, drinking too little water can actually bring on cramping.

EQUIPPING YOURSELF

With water exercise equipment you can alter your workouts to add variety, increase intensity, or recover from injury. All equipment utilizes buoyancy, weight, or resistance (or a combination of these principles). Resistance and flotation tools, such as water jugs, webbed gloves, paddles, plastic plates, floats, boots, or bells, let you increase your work load as you become more fit or reduce impact to prevent or rehabilitate injury. Various commercial devices are available, or you can spare your budget by recycling household items into resourceful water workout equipment. Aquatic exercise specialist Ruth Sova developed guidelines for adding equipment to workout programs in a 1992 article in the Aquatic Exercise Association newsletter. The following guidelines are based on Ruth's recommendations.

Adding Equipment

Before you try to use water exercise equipment to enhance your workout, be sure you're thoroughly familiar with how your body moves in water.

The weightlessness of exercising in water requires a whole new set of muscle "memories" (reflexes and automatic responses) for you to adequately control your movements and predict your body's response in the aquatic environment. Once you have adapted to it, carefully consider which kind of equipment best suits your needs and objectives.

To prevent injury during deep-water aerobics, choose the type of flotation device that is best for you: empty gallon jugs or manufactured flotation cuffs if you do not experience neck or shoulder pain; upper arm cuffs or Body Buoy flotation bubbles if you have not developed proficient torso muscles; a flotation belt if you have a relatively strong torso and want to include upper body aerobic movements; foot or ankle flotation cuffs if you have a very strong torso and seek a nonimpact challenge; or the Wet Vest if you need maximum comfort and stability.

For muscle strength and toning, your choices in resistance equipment range from webbed gloves and water weights to hand-held water resistors and lower leg attachments. To prevent injury and maximize your success, take these precautions for building strength and toning muscles with water exercise equipment:

1. Add water resistance equipment gradually, after you have established a basic level of strength without equipment. Going too far too fast will result in discomfort or even injury, and it will set you back rather than quicken your progress.

2. Always warm up and stretch first, and follow every strengthening routine with flexibility cool-down stretches to avoid soreness and injuries that can result from overly tight muscles.

3. Proper body alignment is always important, but using equipment increases the chance that faulty position and technique will result in injury. Use the positioning guidelines described in the "Injury Prevention Checklist" on pages 21 through 25.

4. Remember that the speed of your movement with resistance equipment determines the intensity level: The faster you push or pull, the heavier the resistance. Each time you use equipment, begin slowly, and gradually add more forceful movements. If you cannot maintain complete control over the movement and your body alignment, you have exceeded your maximum appropriate speed. Always use careful placement; never fling the equipment.

5. To protect your joints, use slower movements when your limbs are straight and faster movements when they are bent. Be sure to keep your elbows and knees bent slightly to avoid "hyperextending" (overstraightening) the joint.

6. Keep the equipment in the water. Moves that begin or end out of the water greatly increase the risk of injury to the joints.

7. Avoid exercises that require you to keep your arms or legs away from your body while you perform repetitive circles. Instead, reduce strain on the ligaments and tendons of your shoulders, knees, hips, back, and elbows by performing repetitions that bring your limbs toward your body instead of holding them away from your body.

8. Short, limited-range movements can cause injury. Choppy movements shorten muscles and only build strength in limited ranges of motion. Concentrate on using the full range of motion around a joint while maintaining proper body alignment; this will build strength throughout the entire range.

Manufacturers produce a wide variety of creative equipment and develop new and better designs all the time. At the top of the "Best Buy" list is the Sprint Exercise/Rehabilitation Flotation Belt (Figure 2.10a), a thoughtfully designed, affordable waist belt that suspends you in deep water for total body aerobic movement without impact shock. The belt is constructed of dense but comfortable foam that does not readily ride up from your waist.

For those seeking greater flotation security and better product durability, the Wet Vest (Figure 2.10b) provides a more expensive and comfortable option that requires somewhat less torso strength for successful vertical balance. Free Floaters, a low-cost alternative worn on the upper arms, also require less torso strength and work well for abdominal exercises. Both the Wet Vest and Free Floaters are frequently used by advanced exercisers and aqua therapists because of their comfort and durability.

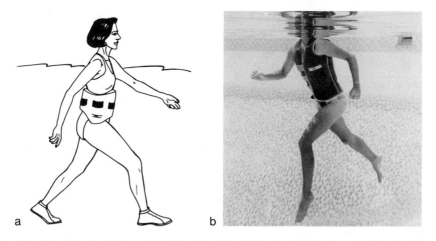

a   b

Figure 2.10 Use a flotation belt for suspension in deep water (a). A wet vest offers great flotation security and helps with vertical balance (b).

The Hydro-Fit system (Figure 2.11a), while somewhat expensive, is perhaps the most versatile choice. Beginners who lack torso strength can wear the flotation cuffs around the upper arms for steady body position. The cuffs can also be linked and worn around the waist by intermediates, or at the ankles by advanced exercisers. The Hydro-Fit kit includes hand-held flotation bells and resistance-increasing webbed gloves. Some webbed glove options last longer and feature a rubber palm for enhanced grip.

HydroTone (Figure 2.11b) supplies the most scientifically enhanced resistance equipment design and adeptly employs the principle of frontal resistance by increasing surface area while allowing water to flow through strategically positioned panels. Competitive athletes, fitness fans, and rehabilitation clients use HydroTone to build strength, power, and endurance in less time than is required for an ordinary workout. Although workouts with HydroTone feel easier and more comfortable than those using most nonaquatic fitness training equipment, the boots and hand-held bells magnify the water's powers and produce impressive strength and conditioning results in people of all ages and abilities. HydroTone comes with complete instructions for specific workout designs.

a   b

Figure 2.11 Beginning, intermediate, or advanced exercisers can benefit from versatile equipment kits (a). Resistance equipment helps build strength, power, and endurance (b).

Aquatic bench stepping (Figure 2.12a) combines the intensity and versatility of stair climbing with the protection of an aquatic environment. The waterproof, sinkable platforms come in several heights and provide an alternative to stair climbing machines or step aerobics. The platform can also be used to alter depths in single-depth pools so that shorter people can perform Supported Squats or the Deep Muscle Buttocks Stretch.

If you travel, the Body Buoy (Figure 2.12b) is a versatile aquatic flotation device that inflates and deflates for storage convenience. Use these relatively inexpensive dual flotation bubbles connected by a strap for deep water exercise or to increase resistance while doing abdominal exercise (see chapter 5).

a   b

Figure 2.12 Sinkable platforms allow water exercisers to achieve fitness results similar to those achieved on land through stair climbing machines and step aerobics (a). Some water equipment can be inflated and deflated for convenient transport and storage (b).

Commercially Available Equipment

Use this guide to learn more about how to choose from the most frequently used commercial water exercise equipment. The recommendations on the use of each type of equipment and suggestions on where to obtain equipment are referenced to the numbered list of manufacturers on pages 44 through 45.

Aqua Shoes. Look for shoes that fit comfortably without binding or crushing the top of your foot. Be sure they fit snugly enough so that they do not slip off when you jump up in the water. Lightweight shoes with good traction add a bit of resistance and a lot of stability. Some shoes are made of wet suit material that helps keep your feet and ankles warm. Contact manufacturer 5, 13, 17, 19, or any of several fitness shoe companies.

Aquatic Steps.   AquaStep makes a waterproof aerobic step platform that is lightweight yet sinks to the pool floor and offers height adjustments. Contact manufacturer 1 or 2.

Flotation Barbells and Cuffs.   Barbells make a good flotation alternative if you do not experience hand, shoulder, neck, or upper back pain. Use them to buoy yourself for lower body exercise, deep water aerobics, or abdominal exercises, or press them through the water in shallow depths to increase upper body resistance and improve muscle fitness. Sprint and Hydro-Fit sell barbells with padded handles. Ankle cuffs fit comfortably over the ankles and provide added resistance to the lower body; some models can be used for advanced deep water exercise in combination with flotation barbells. Contact manufacturer 3, 5, 8, 9, 13, 17, or 19.

Body Ball.   This tossable, squeezable exercise ball floats and is used to strengthen and tone muscles. Contact manufacturer 14.

Body Buoy.   The Body Buoy is great for travel. It consists of two vinyl balloons connected by a fabric strap and can be used in several different positions. It's inflatable, so you can fold it up to pack it away in a small area. Watch out for sharp plastic edges. Contact manufacturer 10.

Chlorine-Resistant Lycra Bodysuits.   If you tend to chill easily, try a full bodysuit with long sleeves and long legs, which are available at reasonable prices from manufacturers 7, 15, 16, and 18. These manufacturers provide sizes and styles for men and women and also offer chlorine-resistant tights and long-sleeved leotards.

Flotation Vests, Belts, and Adult Water Wings.   Flotation for deep-water exercise varies from simple belts and arm hoops to convertible cuffs to therapeutic vests. Two of the best for comfort, price, and function are the Wet Belt from Bioenergetics and the Exercise/Rehab Belt from Sprint-Rothhammer International. Bioenergetics also manufacturers the durable and comfortable Wet Vest. Sprint supplies inexpensive adult water wings, worn on the upper arms. Aquarobics' Free Floaters, soft foam rings that fit over your upper arms, are more comfortable and supportive than water wings. Sprint sells Schwimm Disks, another foam arm hoop alternative. Hydro-Fit offers convertible upper arm cuffs that can be easily fashioned into a flotation belt or ankle cuffs. Contact manufacturer 3, 4, 5, 6, 8, 9, 11, 12, 13, 15, 17, or 19.

HydroTone Boots and Bells.   HydroTone offers a proven system that greatly magnifies the resistance of movement through water. The equipment enhances exercise for all the major muscles of the body including the heart. The degree of resistance automatically changes with the amount of effort or force you apply. To try this highly effective mode of water exercise, contact manufacturer 11.

Paddles.   Several manufacturers offer various types of water resistance enhancement paddles designed to increase your strength training results. Contact manufacturer 5, 13, 17, or 19.

Water Wrist Weights.   Waterproof wrist weights come in several weights. Use them to enhance upper body toning even when the arms are elevated out of the water. Not recommended for use during aerobic exercise or other quick movements. Contact manufacturer 4, 13, 17, or 19.

Webbed Gloves.   Water gloves create a webbed hand to increase the water's resistance to your upper body movements. Use webbed gloves to enhance upper body muscle endurance and strength and to intensify your aerobic workout. Contact manufacturer 9, 13, 17, or 19.

Equipment Distributors and Manufacturers

1. Aerobic Workbench
   P.O. Box 2237
   Largo, Florida 34640
   (813) 391-7419

2. AquaStep
   280 Elizabeth St., A110
   Atlanta, Georgia 30307
   (404) 522-6202

3. Aquarobics
   P.O. Box 5732
   Greenville, South Carolina 29606
   (803) 235-4066

4. Aqua Source
   6112 North Covington
   Oklahoma City, Oklahoma 73132
   (405) 722-2651

5. Aquatic Exercise Products
   3070 Kerner Blvd., Unit S
   San Rafael, California 94901
   (415) 485-5323

6. Bioenergetics
   2790 Montgomery Hwy.
   Pelham, Alabama 35124
   (800) 433-2627
   (214) 350-1333

7. Clingons Activewear
   P.O. Box 721
   Millersville, Maryland 21108
   (800) 755-7572

8. Excel Sports Science
   P.O. Box 5612
   Eugene, Oregon 97405

   (800) 922-9544
   (503) 484-2454

9. Hydro-Fit
   440 Charmelton St.
   Eugene, Oregon 97401

   (800) 346-7295
   (503) 484-4361

10. Hydrorobics (Body Buoys)
    158 Edgewood Ave.
    Atlanta, Georgia 30303

    (404) 321-6864

11. HydroTone International
    3535 N.W. 58th St., Suite 935
    Oklahoma City, Oklahoma 73112

    (800) 622-8663
    (405) 789-7717

12. Jun Konno
    378-1-453 Aricho Hodogayaku
    Yokahama, Japan 240

    (045) 381-8605

13. Recreonics
    7696 Zionsville Rd.
    Indianapolis, Indiana 46268

    (800) 428-3254
    (317) 872-4400

14. SportClub
    615 W. Johnson Ave., Bldg. #3
    Cheshire, Connecticut 06410

    (800) 345-3610
    (203) 271-1156

15. Speedo Activewear
    7911 Haskell Avenue
    Van Nuys, California 91409

    (800) 547-8770

16. Sport Europa
    7871 N.W. 15th St.
    Miami, Florida 33126

    (800) 327-7031
    (305) 477-5520

17. Sprint-Rothhammer International
    P.O. Box 5579
    Santa Maria, California 93456

    (800) 235-2156
    (805) 481-2744

18. WaterWear
    P.O. Box 687
    Wilton, New Hampshire 03086

    (800) 321-7848
    (603) 654-9885

19. World of Service
    52/58 Albert Road
    Luton, Beds, England LU13PR

    (0582) 415-214

Fashioning Equipment From Household Items

Many common household items make excellent and inexpensive water workout equipment. The following are examples of exercise apparatuses that can be fashioned inexpensively from common household items.

Kids' Kick Boards.   Use them to work the upper body in push/pull exercises. Small kick boards offer increased surface area and buoyancy over plates, so start with no equipment, later add the plates, and graduate to kick boards when you need more resistance.

Old Lightweight Canvas Sneakers.   Wear your clean old lightweight canvas sneakers in place of aqua shoes for traction and stability.

Plastic Jugs.   Empty plastic jugs with caps provide cost-free flotation for deep-water exercises and can be used to increase the resistance of abdominal exercises. Be sure to soak off the labels first to protect the pool filter. If you use milk jugs, wash them out with hot, soapy water first, let them dry with covers off, and then resecure the caps.

Plastic Picnic Plates or Frisbees.   Wash your family's plastic picnic plates and reuse them for added resistance during upper body exercises. Or use the frozen dinner plates (without sections) that come with some microwave dinners. Frisbees also work well. Be sure to start with the smaller sizes first; you can graduate to the larger Frisbees as your strength develops. The two disks must be of identical size and density to ensure balanced muscle conditioning and prevent injury.

SELECTING APPROPRIATE MUSIC

Music can motivate and stimulate you to get more out of your workouts. Its smooth, continuous rhythms can help map your program from Warm-Up, through Aerobic Exercise, Muscle Strengthening and Toning, and Final Cool-Down. Often music can give you the impetus to continue on to the end of your program instead of giving up. This music selection guide will help those who wish to exercise to music.

Select songs that have upbeat energy: songs that are full of life and make you want to dance. Your exercise routine will be more fun if your movements interpret the music. For instance, the chorus has been described as "where the song blossoms." Bloom into an especially lively pattern of exercises during the chorus and repeat the pattern each time the chorus returns. The music's energy gives you the right kind of motivation for each particular section: Invigorating energy motivates you for aerobics, while soothing energy encourages you to decrease intensity for aerobic cool-down or to soften and relax your muscles for final stretch.

Sometimes the energy stimulation music provides is more important than adhering to tempo. Some older adults and individuals with movement limitations need to move at the speed that is most comfortable to them at the moment. In that case, let the music entertain you rather than dictate your movement tempo. Nonrhythmic relaxation music, or recordings of bird songs, crickets, wind, rain, or waterfalls can provide a pleasant, stimulating background for nonrhythmic movement.

Finding a Tempo

The *beats per minute* in a piece of music determine the tempo of your exercise. A simple way to determine the beats per minute in your favorite music is to follow these steps:

1. Find a digital watch or clock that tracks seconds, play your music, and tap your feet in time to the tempo.
2. Count the number of taps your foot makes in 15 seconds.
3. Multiply that number by four.

The result is the number of beats per minute in that song.

Table 2.3 tells you more about matching the right energy, beats per minute, and length to each section. Note that the tempo gradually increases, then decreases during the aerobics section, and maintains a steady beat during the calisthenics. If you are just starting out, have arthritis, are overweight, or recently have recovered from injury, be sure to use the slower tempos.

Table 2.3
Set Your Routine To Music

Section	Beats per minute	# of minutes	Energy
Thermal Warm-Up	125-135	3-5	Stimulating
Warm-Up Stretch	100-135	3-5	Flowing but stimulating
Pre-aerobic (optional calisthenics)	115-130	3-5	Invigorating

Aerobic Exercise Phase

Use a tempo that gradually increases, then gradually decreases, for the safest response from your heart, lungs, and circulatory system. Interval training, in which you alternate the tempo between faster and slower, is a method that highly fit exercisers can use to vary their workouts.

Warm-up aerobic	120-135	3-5	Invigorating
Intermediate aerobic	130-145	3-5	Invigorating
Peak intensity	145-155	3-10	High energy
Intermediate aerobic	130-145	3-5	Invigorating

(continued)

Table 2.3 *(continued)*

Section	Beats per minute	# of minutes	Energy
Cool-down aerobic	120-135	3-5	Stimulating and soothing
Calisthenics (muscle strength-ening and toning exercises)	115-135	10-20	Rhythmic and stimulating
Final Cool-Down Stretch	90-110	5-10	Soothing

Safety Considerations

Avoid using plug-in appliances near the pool. Battery operated portable cassette players are safer, and several manufacturers offer rechargeable players. If you use a plug-in appliance, be sure it is five or more feet from the pool and elevated on a nonmetallic table or shelf, and that your power cord is free from frays or exposed areas. Do not plug in, unplug, or use appliances while standing in a puddle.

If you must use a plug-in appliance near the pool, buy a ground-fault circuit interrupter (GFCI), a device designed to prevent electrocution that can be purchased for as little as (U.S.) $15 from hardware and electrical supply stores. It comes as either a portable adapter for plugging into an outlet or as a replacement for the outlet.

PART
II

Performing Water Exercises

Part I gave you the background necessary to prepare you to learn the water workout exercises and create a thoroughly satisfying water workout. The exercises illustrated in chapters 3, 4, 5, and 6 take you through the complete Basic Water Workout sequence from Thermal Warm-Up and Warm-Up Stretch through Aerobic Exercises, Muscle Strengthening and Toning, and the Final Cool-Down Stretch. The Basic Water Workout is designed for individuals who currently have a basic level of fitness (see "Initial Conditioning Stage," page 20) and who have no special concerns or advanced objectives (see chapter 7, "Creating Your Fitness Plan"). Before you begin any of the water workout sequences, familiarize yourself with the wide variety of balanced moves and stretches illustrated in this chapter. Then get in the pool and follow the condensed sequence in chapter 7 entitled "Your First Water Workout."

Use the "Injury Prevention Checklist" in chapter 2 to review the fundamentals of injury prevention.

After completing Your First Water Workout one or more times, move on to the Basic Water Workout, a thorough, balanced exercise session that will leave you feeling refreshed, energized, and limber. Perform the exercises in the order listed. The Warm-Up and Aerobic Exercises are in a sequence designed to raise and then lower your intensity gradually. The flexibility exercises are arranged in an order that makes it easy and comfortable to stretch all the major muscle groups and to move smoothly from region to region. The order of exercises for Muscle Strengthening and Toning follows the strength training principle that you exercise the larger muscle groups of each body area first, then the smaller muscles. This allows you to complete the most demanding exercises when you are the least fatigued.

In some cases you may wish to pick and choose your exercises. Nevertheless, you should retain the order listed rather than jump around, and you should strive to perform all stretches in both the warm-up and cool-down phases. Try to build up gradually until you can complete every aerobic and muscle toning exercise for a balanced workout, but eliminate any exercises that you find too cumbersome or uncomfortable.

On some days you may wish to perform a shorter workout or focus on different aspects. For instance, if mental relaxation or increased flexibility is a primary goal, try completing the Thermal Warm-Up and Warm-Up Stretches routine found in chapter 3 without performing the exercises outlined in chapters 4 and 5. If you are basically fit and wish to concentrate on aerobic conditioning one day and muscle strengthening and toning the next, you can complete the entire Warm-Up (chapter 3) and either an aerobics-only workout (Water Aerobics, chapter 4) or a calisthenics-only workout (Water Exercises to Strengthen and Tone, chapter 5) followed by the complete Final Cool-Down (chapter 6). For overall fitness, try to work up gradually to three water aerobics workouts and two muscle strengthening and toning workouts per week, starting each workout with the Warm-Up and finishing each with the Final Cool-Down. Be sure to space out your aerobic workouts; allow one day between strength workouts for best results.

CHAPTER

3

Warm-Up

Prepare your body for more challenging exercise by starting with a mild, gradually building rhythmic warm-up to increase blood flow and warm the muscles before stretching. Let the refreshing environment of the pool wake up your senses and generate your enthusiasm. Then complete a light stretch routine to lengthen the muscles prior to your aerobic and muscle toning activity. The Thermal Warm-Up and Stretches Warm-Up should be performed in numerical order at the beginning of every workout session and should generally take about 10 minutes. Begin in waist- to chest-deep water. Throughout the warm-up and your entire water workout, concentrate on bracing your spine in the neutral position by contracting your abdominals and buttocks. In exercises where bracing to protect your spine is particularly important, the bracing reminder has been repeated. Most individuals should avoid use of resistive equipment during the Thermal Warm-Up.

THERMAL WARM-UP
(5 minutes)

Move #1: Water Walk

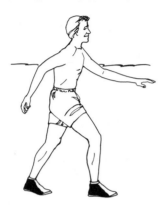

Starting Position: Stand with your abdominal muscles firm, tailbone pointed toward the floor, buttocks tucked somewhat to brace your spine in position, shoulders back, and chest lifted (neutral position).

Action: Stride or jog forward eight steps, then back four steps. Maintain the neutral position throughout the exercise. Push relatively straight arms forward and back at your sides as you walk. Turn your hands each time so that the palms press against the water. Use your arms *in opposition* to your legs: When you step forward with your right leg, bring your left arm forward, and vice versa.

Variations:

- Walk forward and backward with short steps, long steps, average steps, or step kicks.
- Move in the pattern of a circle or square.

  When you are ready to increase intensity:
- Stride by taking very large, controlled steps.
- Bound by pushing off with your back foot to bounce up off the pool floor between strides.

Safety Tip: When circling, be sure to turn around midway and circle in the other direction to balance the physical demands on your body.

Move #2: Pedal Jog

Action: Instead of lifting your whole foot from the floor as you would when running, alternately lift one heel, then the other. Pump your arms in opposition to your legs.

Move #3: Pomp & Circumstance
Action:

1. Pretend you are graduating. Take one long step forward with your right leg. Swing your opposite arm forward from the shoulder, palm first.
2. Next, step together: Bring your left foot forward to meet the right foot. Return your arm to your side, palm facing back.
3. Then take one long step forward with your left leg. Bring your opposite arm forward from the shoulder, palm first.
4. Step together: Bring your right foot forward to meet your left foot. Return your arm to your side, palm facing back.

Perform the same exercise backwards to cross the pool in the opposite direction. Repeat, moving forward 8 steps and back 8 steps.

Move #4: Knee Lift Jog/March

Action: Alternately lift one knee, then the other, moving your arms and legs in opposition to each other to elevate your body responses and increase body temperature. (Lift your right knee and your left arm. Put your foot down and bring your arm back to your side. Lift your left knee and your right arm. Put your foot down and bring your arm back to your side.)

Variations:

- Jog: Jog in place, hopping from foot to foot.
- March: Eliminate the hop between movements to reduce the intensity or the impact shock of this exercise. As you become more fit, gradually build the intensity, starting with low lifts or slow lifts, then building to "double time" and lifting your knees as high as feels comfortable.

Safety Tips: Keep your spine braced between contracted abdominals and buttocks to protect your lower back. Avoid lifting your knees beyond hip height. Start with the legs first and add the arms in later, when you have mastered the legs.

Move #5: Toy Soldier March

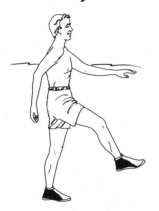

Action: March with straight legs.

1. Lift your right leg from the hip, knee straight. At the same time, reach forward with your left arm. Put your foot down and bring your arm to your side.
2. Lift your left leg from the hip, knee straight. At the same time, reach forward with your right arm. Put your foot down and bring your arm to your side.

Safety Tips: Start with the legs first and add the arms in later, when you have mastered the legs. Keep your pelvis aligned by bracing your spine between contracted abdominal and buttocks muscles.

Move #6: Can-Can Kicks

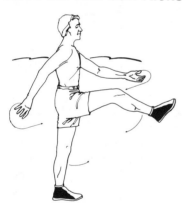

Action:

1. Brace the position of your spine by contracting your abdominal and buttocks muscles. Kick your right leg forward, contracting your abdominals as you lift your leg from the hip, like a football punter. At the same time, swing your opposite arm forward from the shoulder, palm first.
2. As you lower your right leg, hop onto your right foot and kick your left leg forward, lifting your leg from the hip. As you swing your right arm forward from the shoulder, palm first, lower your left arm to your side. Determine the height of the kick based on what is most comfortable for you; keep all kicks below hip height.

Alternate kicks for 8 to 16 repetitions.

Safety Tip: If you have ever experienced chronic back pain, keep your kicks low.

Move #7: Kick Up Your Heels

Starting Position: Stand with your feet about shoulder-width apart.

Action:

1. Pull in your abdominals. Reach forward with your right arm and lift your right heel toward your buttocks, keeping your thighs parallel to each other and perpendicular to the floor.
2. Return your arm and leg to starting position.
3. Brace your torso position. Reach forward with your left arm and lift your left heel toward your buttocks, keeping your thighs parallel to each other and perpendicular to the floor.
4. Return your arm and leg to starting position.

Repeat 16 times.

Variations: To increase intensity, do the exercise without placing one foot down before lifting the other; instead, jump from foot to foot as you kick up each heel.

Move #8: Side Knee Hop

Starting Position: Stand with your feet shoulder-width apart, arms out in front of your chest.

Action:

1. Hop and lift your right knee up and out to the right while you press your palms out to either side.
2. Hop and bring your feet together, putting your foot back on the floor. At the same time, press your palms toward one another, arms outstretched in front of your chest.
3. Hop and lift your left knee up and out to the side while you press your palms out to either side.
4. Hop and bring your feet together, putting your foot back down on the floor. At the same time, press your palms toward one another, arms outstretched in front of your chest.

Repeat 8 to 16 times.

Variation: Eliminate the small hop between movements to reduce the intensity or the impact shock of this exercise.

Move #9: Heel Jacks

Starting Position: Begin with your hands at your sides, feet together.

Action:

1. Kick your right leg out to the side and place your right heel on the pool floor, pointing your toe toward the ceiling. At the same time, press both palms outward from your sides.
2. Bring both feet back together and press your palms toward your sides.
3. Kick your left leg out to the side and place your left heel on the pool floor. Press both palms outward from your sides.
4. Bring both feet back together and press your palms toward your sides.

Repeat 8 to 16 times.

Variation: Add a small hop onto both feet at once between each movement to increase the intensity of this exercise.

Move #10: Alternate Leg Press Backs

Starting Position: Start with feet together, arms at your sides. Pull in your abdominals and buttocks to brace your spine.

Action:

1. Press both arms straight out in front, scooping forward with your palms as you press your right leg all the way back behind you.
2. Bring both feet back together again and scoop your palms back toward your sides.
3. Again, press both arms straight out in front, scooping forward with your palms as you press your left leg all the way behind you.
4. Bring both feet back together again and scoop your palms back toward your sides. Remember to breathe deeply.

Repeat sequence 8 to 16 times.

Variations: Add a small hop between movements to increase the intensity of this exercise. If you are prone to knee or back pain, or seek greater stability, eliminate the bounce and perform this exercise facing the pool wall or ladder and hold on with both hands.

Safety Tips: Concentrate on keeping your front knee over your heel rather than over your toes. Brace your pelvis firmly in the neutral position by contracting your abdominal and buttocks muscles.

Move #11: Knee Lift Kick

Starting Position: Begin with your feet shoulder-width apart, hands at your sides. Pull in your abdominals and squeeze your buttocks to brace your spine.

Action:

1. Lift your right knee toward your chest, no higher than hip height. At the same time, reach your opposite arm forward from the shoulder, palm first.
2. Then kick your right leg forward from the knee.
3. Bend your knee, then return your foot to the floor of the pool and bring your arm to your side.

Repeat the sequence with the left leg and right arm.

Repeat sequence 8 times.

Variation: Add a small hop between movements to increase the intensity of this exercise.

Safety Tip: As you kick forward, be sure to maintain a slight bend at the knee to eliminate hyperextension. Avoid this exercise if you have a tendency to experience knee pain.

WARM-UP STRETCHES
(5 minutes)

Stretching Technique: Stretch each major muscle group carefully to prepare the body for exercise and to prevent injury. The instructions are designed to move you smoothly and continuously from stretch to stretch in the order listed. As you become more familiar with the stretches, you may change the sequence to add variety, but be sure to stretch the muscle group near to the one you just finished stretching to help prevent muscle tears.

During the Warm-Up Stretches, hold each static stretch position for 8 to 10 seconds (avoid bouncing). At the end of your workout, hold each Final Cool-Down Stretch for 20 to 30 seconds. Remember to stretch only to the point where you feel a comfortable degree of resistance. If you feel pain or discomfort, you are either stretching too far (ease up on the stretch and allow your muscle to relax) or you are out of position (double check the instructions and illustration).

If you like, you can continuously move your arms through the water while stretching the lower body to keep your muscles supple and your body comfortably warm. But if your shoulder joints are tender or vulnerable, you may want to minimize such arm movements during your stretch programs. You can also march or pedal jog in place to stay warm while you stretch the upper body if you are able to keep your stretch and body position stable while doing so.

Lower Body Stretches

Perform the first nine stretches at pool side (Outer Thigh Stretch through Hamstring Stretch). Complete all nine while holding on to the pool edge with your left hand unless instructed otherwise. Then turn around and complete the same stretches for the other side of the body while holding on to the pool edge with your right hand.

Move #12: Outer Thigh Stretch

Starting Position: Stand with your left side toward the pool wall, holding on to the pool edge with your left hand.

Action: Stand up straight and cross your outside leg over the leg nearest to the side of the pool. Reach out toward the middle of the pool with your free arm and lean your hip in toward the pool edge. Optional: Cup your hand and press your palm toward the wall. Turn your palm around and press away from the wall. Repeat this arm action slowly, in time to the music if you are using it. Relax the muscles on the outside of your left thigh and hold the stretch position, without bouncing, for approximately 10 seconds, or for about 16 beats of the music (remember: 10 seconds for Warm-Up Stretches; 20 to 30 seconds for Cool-Down Stretches).

Safety Tips: Try to keep both shoulders relaxed and at an even height. Be sure to contract your abdominals firmly and stand up straight, or the position could put strain on your lower back. Breathe deeply to encourage the muscles to relax.

Move #13: Lower Back Stretch with Ankle Rotation

Starting Position: Hold on to the pool edge. Stand up straight and firmly contract your abdominal muscles.

Action: Lift your right leg. Reaching your arm behind your thigh, draw your knee toward your chest as you relax your lower back. Slowly roll your foot in a circle counterclockwise for several revolutions. Then roll it clockwise. Rotate the ankle through your full range of motion. (Roll it in as wide a circle as possible without causing pain.)

Lean forward from the hips with a flat back and relax your lower back.

Move #14: Front of Thigh Stretch

Starting Position: Turn your back to the wall and stand about 18 inches or 1/2 meter from it. Hold on to the pool edge with your outstretched left arm and place your left foot on the wall behind you.

Action: Standing up straight, squeeze your abdominal muscles in tight and push your hips away from the wall so that your knee joint forms a right angle. Breathe deeply and relax the front of your thigh.

Safety Tip: Be sure to pull in your abdominals, contract your buttocks slightly, and point your tailbone toward the floor to keep your spine aligned.

Move #15: Shin Stretch and Shoulder Shrug

Starting Position: Turn your body so that you are standing with your left side toward the pool wall.

Action: Cross your outside leg over your inside leg. Point your toes and place the tops of your toes on the floor of the pool. Breathe deeply and relax your shin.

While you stretch your shins, slowly raise both shoulders toward your ears, then slowly depress your shoulders. Repeat slowly in time to the music.

Move #16: Inner Thigh Step Out

Starting Position: Stand with both feet on the floor.

Action: Step out to the side, bending your left knee and moving your right leg as far from your torso as you find comfortable. Relax your inner thigh, hold a steady, nonbouncing stretch, and breathe deeply. Optional: To stay warm, press your palm toward the pool wall, then away from it in time to the music.

Safety Tip: Keep your bent knee positioned over your heel to prevent undue pressure at the knee joint. If your knee is pushing out over your toes, put your feet wider apart.

Move #17: Hip Flexor Stretch

Starting Position: Hold on to the pool edge and pivot turn on your toes to face the pool wall. Stand with one foot in front of the other at a comfortable distance.

Action: With your front knee bent, straighten your back leg, and raise your back heel (you are on the toes of your back foot). Pull in your abdominals and gently press your hips down and forward to stretch the hip flexor muscles that run from your torso to the front of your thigh. Optional: With your free hand (the one not holding the pool edge) press your palm toward the pool wall, then away from it in time to the music.

Safety Tip: Keep your bent knee positioned over your heel to prevent undue pressure at the knee joint. Place your feet wider apart from front to back if your knee is pushing out over your toes.

Move #18: Straight Leg Calf Stretch

Starting Position: After the Hip Flexor Stretch (Move #17), you are standing with one foot in front of the other. Move your back foot a bit closer to the front foot.

Action: Press your heel down to the floor. Be sure that your back foot is pointing straight ahead and that your front knee is over your heel rather than over your toes. Relax your calf muscle at the back of your lower leg. Optional: Press your other palm toward the pool wall, then away from it in time to the music.

Safety Tip: If your calf muscle feels tight and uncomfortable, or if you have difficulty relaxing the calf muscle, bring your back foot a little closer to the front foot until you can press your heel to the floor comfortably. When your calf muscles are tight you may tend to splay your foot out to the side. To perform this stretch properly, you must have your back foot pointed straight ahead, not out to the side.

Move #19: Bent Knee Calf Stretch

Starting Position: Stand with one foot in front of the other.

Action: Bring your back foot another step closer to the front foot. Bend your back knee. Continue to support your weight on the front leg. Relax your calf muscle and Achilles tendon. Optional: Press one palm toward the pool wall, then away from it in time to the music. Be sure to complete both the Straight Leg Calf Stretch (Move #18) and the Bent Knee Calf Stretch (Move #19). Both stretches are necessary because of the structural arrangement of the lower leg. The second calf stretch helps prevent Achilles tendonitis. Keep your abdominals and buttocks contracted firmly to brace the position of your spine.

Move #20: Hamstring Stretch

Starting Position: Face the pool wall.

Action: Place your right foot against the wall at a height that allows you to straighten your leg comfortably without locking or hyperextending the knee. Pull in your abdominals, keep your back flat, and lean forward from the hip. Relax and soften the muscles at the back of your thigh. Hold on to the pool edge for stability.

Safety Tips: Keep a very slight bend at the knee of the leg you are stretching. Flatten your back rather than rounding it to ensure that the hamstring receives a proper stretch.

Switch sides: Turn around, hold the pool edge with the opposite hand, and repeat the lower body sequence (Moves #12 through #20) to stretch the other side.

Healthy Back Stretches

Flexible lower body muscles help prevent or minimize low back pain. Here are three more stretches to encourage a healthy back.

Move #21: Deep Muscle Buttocks Stretch

Starting Position: Face the pool wall with both hands on the edge.

Action: Cross your left ankle at your right knee and slowly lower yourself as if you were sitting in a chair. Relax your buttocks, hip, and outer thigh; contract your abdominal muscles; and breathe deeply. Hold the stretch for 10 seconds (warm-up) or 20 to 30 seconds (cool-down). Put both feet on the floor and stand up, then repeat the stretch with your right ankle at your left knee.

Move #22: Full Back Stretch

Starting Position: Continue facing the pool wall with both hands holding on to the edge.

Action: Lower yourself into the water and place your feet more than shoulder-width apart against the wall. The water will buoy your body. Relax and soften the muscles of your entire back.

Move #23: Mid-Back Stretch

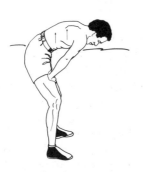

Starting Position: Stand in waist- to chest-deep water with your feet more than shoulder-width apart and your knees bent and over your heels. Stand near the edge of the pool with your side toward the pool wall.

Action:

1. To support your body weight, place both hands on the tops of your thighs, midway between hip and knee. Lean forward and look at the bottom of the pool. Take a deep breath, then exhale and arch your back upward toward the sky as you contract your abdominals and buttocks. Breathing deeply, hold the position for 10 seconds and relax your back (20 to 30 seconds for Cool-Down Stretch). Then press yourself up slowly with your hands on your thighs to prevent stress to your low back.

2. Keep your knees bent. Reach both hands toward the wall and lightly grasp the pool edge with both hands (or place one hand on the arm closest to the wall if this is too far to stretch). Breathe fully and evenly as you hold the position for 10 seconds and "soften" the muscles of your back (20 to 30 seconds for Cool-Down Stretch). Be sure to keep your hips facing straight ahead, not twisted toward the pool wall.

3. Bring your feet closer together to about shoulder-width apart. Reach both hands toward the wall and grasp the pool edge with both hands (or place one hand on the arm closest to the wall if this is too far to stretch). Breathe fully and evenly as you hold the position for 10 seconds and "soften" the muscles of your back (20 to 30 seconds for Cool-Down Stretch). Be sure to keep your hips facing straight ahead, not twisted toward the pool wall.

4. Turn around and repeat steps 1 through 3.

Upper Body Stretches

Now step away from the wall and perform these additional upper body stretches.

Move #24: Elbow Press Back

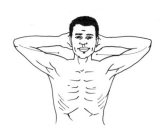

Starting Position: Stand with your feet shoulder-width apart, in the neutral position. Place your hands gently behind your neck, elbows in front.

Action: Perform this exercise very slowly: Press both elbows back as you squeeze the muscles of your shoulder blades, and take a deep breath. Exhale slowly as you bring the elbows toward each other. Repeat 4-8 times.

Safety Tip: Avoid pressing your head forward as you press your elbows back.

Move #25: Chest Stretch with Shoulder Rolls

Starting Position: Stand with your feet shoulder-width apart, in the neutral position.

Action: 1. Before you stretch your chest, raise both shoulders up toward your ears. Roll them backward as you bring your shoulder blades together. Then lower your shoulders and roll them forward. Repeat 8 to 16 times.

2. Contract your abdomen and roll your shoulders back. Bring both hands backward, clasp them behind your back, and gently stretch your chest. Breathe deeply and hold the stretch for 10 seconds (20-30 for Cool-Down Stretch).

Move #26: Upper Back Stretch

Action: Bring your arms forward, reach out in front of your chest, and link your thumbs. While standing up straight, contract your abdominal muscles, round your upper back, and look down at the floor of the pool. Relax the muscles of your upper back, neck, and shoulders. Be sure to keep your shoulders down.

Move #27: Torso and Shoulder Stretch

Action: Contract your abdominal and buttocks muscles to brace your spine. Bring your arms out to the sides. Then raise your arms overhead and link your thumbs together. Lift your chest as you reach toward the sky. Flex the knees slightly and bring your arms next to your ears being careful not to arch your back or drop your head. Breathe deeply and hold the stretch for 16 counts.

Safety Tips: Keep your elbows slightly bent to avoid stressing the elbow joint. If your shoulders feel tight, lower your hands in front of your face until the tightness disappears.

Move #28: Shoulder and Upper Arm Stretch

Action:

1. Reach behind your neck with your right hand.
2. Clasp your right elbow with the left hand. Draw your right elbow toward your head, just to the point of comfortable resistance. Relax your shoulder and upper arm. Keep your head up straight to protect your neck.
3. Extend your right arm.
4. Repeat the sequence with the left arm to stretch the other side.

Safety Tips: Avoid tipping your head forward. Change the position of your supporting arm (bring it in front of your face) if your head is being forced forward.

4

Water Aerobics

G et lively and enjoy the unique feeling of moving about briskly in the aquatic environment. Remember to follow an aerobic progression like the one in Table 2.2 on pages 29 through 30. Gradually introduce your heart, lungs, and circulatory system to the increase in exertion with an aerobic warm-up that emphasizes continuous movement using the larger muscle groups and elevates the heart rate gradually. Start with low intensity aerobic activity (perceived exertion: fairly light). As you progress into the aerobics segment, the activity and your heart rate should build gradually to peak intensity (perceived exertion: somewhat hard or hard). The aerobic cool-down reduces intensity gradually, allowing the cardiovascular system to gradually return to equilibrium, the way it functioned before you began aerobic exertion, to prevent injury and cardiac complications. By the end of the aerobic section, your heart rate should be at the low end of your target zone, and your perceived exertion should be fairly light.

As a reminder, you can change your level of intensity in several ways:

- Vary the size of the movement. The larger the movement, the greater the water's resistance and the higher the intensity. Take larger steps to increase or smaller steps to decrease intensity.

- Increase your movement to and from different locations in the pool (side-to-side, circle, back-and-forth) to elevate your heart rate. Stay in one place to lower your intensity.
- Increase or decrease speed of movement to raise or lower the amount of force needed to push your body through the water.
- Increase or decrease the surface area you are pushing through the water. For instance, cupped hands resist more water than balled fists or slices. Figure 4.1 shows the three hand position options used to vary intensity. Keep your hands under water during all the moves (unless otherwise indicated) to work against the water and to prevent injury caused by abrupt changes in resistance.

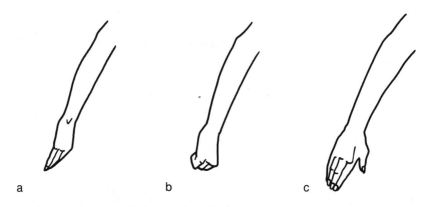

a   b   c

Figure 4.1   Cup your hands to increase the intensity of resistance to your upper body (a). Fold your hand into a fist to reduce the intensity (b). Slice your hand sideways through the water to minimize resistance (c).

The aerobic sequence described in this chapter begins with an essential warm-up sequence that repeats the exercises in the Thermal Warm-Up but requires you to gradually increase the intensity higher than you would during the initial warm-up. Then it takes you through a progressive sequence to peak intensity and finally cools you down by returning you to the exercises used in the warm-up sections. Here you can pick and choose the exercises you like and add more later for variety. Older adults or individuals who have been inactive may find the Older Adult, First Water Workout, or other exercise sequences for special concerns found in chapter 7 more appropriate. During peak aerobics, choose from shallow-water exercises and deep-water moves that use flotation equipment. Practice the leg movements first, then add the arms when you are ready. Again, avoid any exercise you find uncomfortable. As you become more fit, you will probably find that you become more proficient and comfortable with most of the exercises.

WARM-UP AEROBICS

First perform the same exercises as those shown in the Thermal Warm-Up (chapter 3), but gradually build to more vigorous intensity. Then add these additional aerobic warm-up exercises.

Move #29: Snake Walk

Starting Position: Pull in your abdominals and contract your buttocks firmly to brace your spine.

Action:
1. Push your body through the water as you stride with large steps. Step forward with your right leg as you reach forward with your left arm. Step forward with your left leg as you reach forward with your right arm.
2. "Snake" around the shallow end, in a curving or winding pattern.

Safety Tip: Push firmly through the water, but move only as swiftly as you can manage with complete control, without wavering or losing your spinal stability.

Move #30: Step Wide Side

Starting Position: Start with your feet together, arms at your sides in waist- to chest-deep water.

Action:
1. Brace your spine and take a big step sideways with your right leg. At the same time, press your palms out to either side.
2. Then step together: Bring your left leg in to meet your right leg. Bring your palms back to your sides. Repeat this sequence and move across the width of the pool. Then repeat the sequence, starting with the left leg, to cross the pool in the opposite direction.

Variation: As you step together, bring your palms toward each other behind your back.

Move #31: Hydro Jacks

Starting Position: Start with your feet shoulder-width apart, hands at your sides, in waist- to chest-deep water.

Action:

1. Brace your spine, then jump up and land in a wide stance with your knees bent and your heels on the pool floor. Toes should be just slightly pointed out to the sides. At the same time, press your palms out to either side. Keep your hands under the water.

2. Jump up and bring your feet together. Land with bent knees. At the same time, press your palms toward each other behind your buttocks.

Repeat full sequence eight times.

Variation: Stride or bound forward and do a Hydro Jack as you move backward with each jump for intensified aerobic conditioning.

Safety Tip: Keep your abdominals pulled in firmly and breathe deeply.

Move #32: Cross-Country Ski

Starting Position: Stand in waist- to chest-deep water. Start with your left foot out in front of your body, right foot back; right arm reaching out in front (but under the water), left arm reaching back. Determine the space between your front and back foot based on comfort. Increase the distance between your feet to increase the intensity.

Action:

1. Brace your spine. Hop up and bring your left leg forward while you press the right leg back in a cross-country ski motion. At the same time, scoop your right palm forward and press your left palm back.

2. Hop up and switch legs and arms again: Bring your right leg forward as you push your left leg back. Scoop your left palm forward as you press your right palm back.

Repeat for 16 sets.

Variations: To increase intensity, instead of skiing in place, propel your body forward and backward with the cross-country ski motion. To decrease intensity, shorten the distance between your front foot and back foot.

Safety Tips: Keep the front knee behind your toes, over your heel, as you land. Keep the abdominals and buttocks contracted to brace and protect your back.

Move #33: Sailor's Jig

Starting Position: Stand on your left foot, right leg lifted out to the side, back braced, and both palms pressed sideways toward your left knee. Begin in waist- to chest-deep water.

Action: Hop from foot to foot for this exercise:

1. Hop onto your right leg as you lift your left leg out to the side. Push both palms, arms straight down, toward the right knee (toward the foot on which you are about to land).

2. Hop onto your left foot while you lift your right leg out to the side. Push both palms, arms straight down, toward the left knee.

Repeat for eight sets.

Variation: For the Knee Lift Jig, hop from foot to foot as you lift your left knee, then your right knee, out to the side.

PEAK INTENSITY AEROBICS

Now that you have gradually increased the level of your aerobic exercise by moving from warm-up moves and gradually building intensity, maintain your peak aerobic level by performing "peak aerobics" exercises. Remember, to raise your level of intensity, increase the size of the movement, travel around the pool, decrease the time it takes to travel from one end of the pool to the other, or enlarge the surface area you are pushing through the water.

Move #34: Jump Forward, Jump Back

Starting Position: Stand in water that reaches to the rib cage or chest. Begin in the neutral position, spine braced, arms extended in front, palms down.

Action:

1. Abdominal Tuck Jump: Jump up lifting both knees, tucking your torso, and squeezing the abdominals firmly while you press your palms backward to move forward.
2. Bring your feet back down, pressing your heels to the floor and bending your knees slightly.
3. Swing your arms forward, palms first, and repeat the abdominal tuck as you jump backward.

Variation: Once you have developed enough abdominal strength and corresponding levels of fitness to perform Jump Forward, Jump Back without risking injury, start with four repetitions at moderate tempo (for example, to music with 130 beats per minute). For variety, jump forward four to eight times then backward four to eight times.

Safety Tips: The jump requires a firm abdominal/buttock contraction and a water power hop that incorporates the push-off training principle of plyometrics. Therefore, it should be performed once you have gained a basic level of fitness and can control the exercise. During these exercises, the abdominal muscles work together with the back, buttocks, and hips for coordinated strength. Keep your abdominals pulled in firmly, even during the jump's descent to avoid hyperextending the lower back and to prevent injury.

Move #35: Mountain Climbing

Starting Position: Move to the pool wall in chest-deep water, face the pool deck, and hold on to the edge with both hands.

Action:

1. Put your right foot against the wall of the pool at a comfortable height and keep the left foot on the floor.
2. Jump up and switch the position of your legs.

Continue for 16 to 32 repetitions.

Safety Tip: Keep your knees slightly bent and your abdominals pulled in firmly. Avoid this exercise if you have neck pain.

Move #36: Ski/Jack Combo

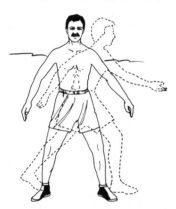

Starting Position: Stand in waist- to chest-deep water. Start with right foot out in front of your body, left foot back; left arm reaching out in front (but under the water), right arm reaching back.

Action:

1. Hop up and bring your left leg forward while you press the right leg all the way back. At the same time, scoop your right palm forward as you press your left palm back.
2. Hop up and switch legs and arms: Bring your right leg forward as you push your left leg back. At the same time, scoop your left palm forward and press your right palm back.
3. Jump out and land in a wide stance with your knees bent and your heels on the pool floor. Toes should be slightly pointed out to the sides. At the same time, press your palms out to either side. Keep your hands under the water.
4. Jump up and bring your feet together. Land with bent knees. At the same time, press your palms toward one another behind your buttocks.

Repeat the full sequence for eight sets.

Safety Tip: Keep your abdominals and buttocks contracted to brace your spine in alignment.

Move #37: Knee Lift Press Backs

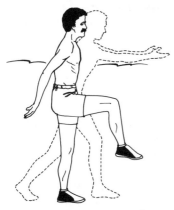

Starting Position: Start with your feet shoulder-width apart, hands at your sides, in waist- to chest-deep water.

Action:

1. Press your palms back behind you as you lift your right knee toward your chest.
2. Bring your palms forward as you press your right leg back behind you. Repeat steps 1 and 2 four times; then bring your feet together.
3. Press your palms behind you and lift your left knee toward your chest.

4. Bring both palms forward as you press your left leg behind you. Repeat steps 3 and 4 four times.

Move #38: Rocking Horse

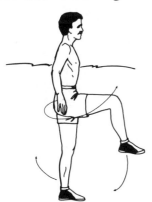

Starting Position: Place your right foot in front of the left foot. Adopt the neutral position.

Action:

1. Standing on your left foot, lift your right knee toward your chest and press both palms down past your hips, arms relatively straight.
2. Hop forward onto the right leg as you kick your left heel up and behind you toward your buttocks. At the same time, swing both arms forward, palms facing up.

Repeat steps 1 and 2 for eight sets.

3. Standing on your right foot, lift your left knee toward your chest and press both palms down past your hips.
4. Hop forward onto the left leg as you kick your right heel up and behind you toward your buttocks. At the same time, press both palms forward.

Repeat steps 3 and 4 for eight sets.

Safety Tips: In this exercise, it is essential that you brace your spine to avoid lower back arching. Hold your abdominals firmly in the tucked position and contract the buttocks. Keep your torso vertical and breathe deeply. Avoid curving the lower back, especially as you kick up your back heel, and do not lean forward and back.

Move #39: Lunge and Center

Starting Position: Start with your hands at your sides, body in the neutral position.

Action:

1. Jump up and turn your torso right as you swing both arms out to the right, palms first. At the same time, squeeze your abdominal muscles and thrust your left leg back.
2. Jump up, turn your torso back to the starting position, and bring both feet together at the center. Bring your arms to your sides.
3. Jump up and turn your torso to the left as you swing both arms out to the left, palms first. At the same time, thrust your right leg back.
4. Jump up, turn your torso back to the starting position, and bring both feet together at the center. Bring your arms to your sides.

Repeat 8 to 16 times.

Variations: To reduce intensity, perform the movements without jumping, and instead pivot on your toes as you press your leg back and turn your torso. Next, step together to bring both feet back to the center.

To increase intensity, between lunges, pull your abdominals in firmly, tuck your torso, and bring both knees toward your chest before bringing your feet together at center. Or bound forward for four repetitions, then Lunge and Center once to each side, bound back for four repetitions, and Lunge and Center once to each side.

Safety Tip: Each time you thrust your leg back, tuck your abdominals in firmly to protect your spine.

Move #40: Lunge Kick Square

Starting Position: Start with your hands at your sides, body in the neutral position.

Action:

1. Lunge right, then left, as in Lunge and Center (Move #39). Propel yourself off the floor by adding a jump between lunges. After the left lunge, remain facing to the left.
2. Kick your right leg forward from the hip, then your left leg.
3. From this position, lunge right, then left. Propel yourself off the floor by adding a jump between lunges. After the left lunge, remain facing to the left.

Repeat the sequence until you have lunged and kicked facing in all four directions. Then repeat, lunging left, then right.

Move #41: Jump Twist

Starting Position: Start in the neutral position with elbows at your waist, hands out in front, palms facing left.

Action:

1. Tuck your torso slightly and push off the bottom of the pool to jump up. While in the air, turn your whole body one-half turn to the right by pressing both palms to the left, elbows at your waist.
2. Coil again and push off the bottom of the pool while you press both palms to the right, elbows at your waist. At the same time, turn your body one-half turn to the left.

Repeat steps 1 and 2 eight times.

Variation: To increase intensity and reduce stress on the low back, first bound forward for four repetitions, then Jump Twist once in each direction; bound back for four repetitions and Jump Twist once in each direction. This allows you to realign your spine between Jump Twists.

Safety Tip: Your torso does not twist during this exercise. Keep your body aligned.

FLOTATION AEROBICS

Flotation equipment will help your workout with the exercises that follow. Choose from this equipment: empty plastic water jugs (covers on), a flotation belt, a vest, and cuffs. Here are some helpful hints.

- Hug the corner of a water jug under each arm, handles out, and place your open palms over the handles (see Figure 4.2a). Avoid using water jugs for flotation if you have neck, shoulder, or upper back pain.
- Flotation belts permit active use of the upper body. Use your arms in opposition to your legs: When your right leg kicks forward, bring your left arm forward, and vice versa (see Figure 4.2b). Tighten the belt snugly enough to keep it from riding up when you move to deep water but loosely enough to permit comfortable breathing.
- Upper arm flotation cuffs give you a greater sense of confidence if flotation belts make you feel unbalanced (see Figure 4.2c). If you have back pain, you may find these cuffs particularly comfortable.

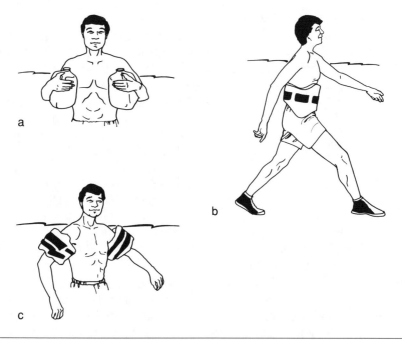

Figure 4.2   Empty plastic gallon or 4-litre water jugs (a), flotation belts (b), and upper arm flotation cuffs (c) increase the benefits of your aerobic workout.

Move #42: Aqua Ski

Equipment: Use a flotation belt, vest, cuffs, or water jugs.

Starting Position: Move to water deep enough to bring your feet off the bottom of the pool. Squeeze your abdominal and buttocks muscles and press your feet down until your legs point straight downward. Then bring your right leg forward and your left leg back. If you are using a flotation belt or vest, press your left arm forward and your right arm back.

Action:

1. Simulate cross-country ski motions. Bring your right leg forward as you thrust the left leg behind you. If you are using a flotation belt or vest, bring your left arm forward at the same time, and push your right arm back. Strive for a full, controlled, and comfortable range of motion instead of using short, quick repetitions. Press the front leg all the way forward, the back leg all the way back.

2. Switch legs and arms.

Repeat 8 to 16 times.

Variations: Keep your knees bent to reduce intensity. Or, for higher intensity, propel your body across the pool. Use cupped palms to pull the water back, and slice your hand through the water when you bring your hand forward.

Safety Tip: Pull in your abdominals firmly and brace your spine with your buttocks muscles to protect your lower back.

Move #43: Floating Side Scissors

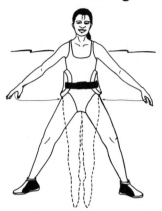

Equipment: Use flotation belt, vest, cuffs, or water jugs.

Starting Position: Move to water deep enough to bring your feet off the pool bottom. Squeeze your abdominal and buttocks muscles and press your feet down until your legs point straight downward.

Action:

1. Bring your legs apart to a comfortable distance. You can bring your arms apart at the same time if you are not using water jugs.

2. Bring your legs together and your hands to your sides.

Repeat 8 to 16 times.

Variation: Bend your knees slightly to increase the water's turbulence and the move's intensity as you push and pull your legs through the water.

Safety Tip: Pull in your abdominals firmly and brace your spine with your buttocks muscles to protect your lower back.

Move #44: Back Float Kick and Squiggle

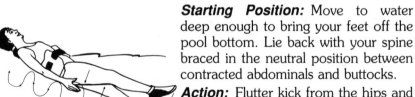
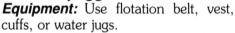

Equipment: Use flotation belt, vest, cuffs, or water jugs.

Starting Position: Move to water deep enough to bring your feet off the pool bottom. Lie back with your spine braced in the neutral position between contracted abdominals and buttocks.

Action: Flutter kick from the hips and propel yourself the length of the pool. Keep your feet under the water. If you are wearing a flotation belt, "squiggle" your arms in an s-like motion at your sides.

Variation: If you don't mind a wet head, you can simulate the backstroke to increase intensity.

Safety Tip: Look over your shoulder periodically to avoid collision with other bathers.

Move #45: Vertical Frog Bob

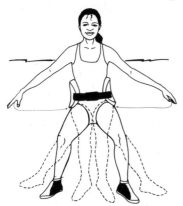

Equipment: Use flotation belt, vest, cuffs, or water jugs.

Starting Position: Move to water deep enough to bring your feet off the pool bottom. Bring your feet down so that your legs point straight downward.

Action:

1. Firmly squeeze your abdominal and buttocks muscles and draw both knees toward your chest. If your hands are free, bring your palms toward each other in front of you as you tuck.

2. Bring your feet wide apart while straightening your legs toward the pool bottom. If your hands are free, press your palms out to the side and down to your sides as you bring your feet apart and straighten your legs.

3. Swiftly glide your legs together.

Repeat the sequence eight times.

Variation: For increased intensity, perform the same exercise horizontally, on your back, and cross the pool.

Safety Tip: Push your feet apart first, so that your knees do not separate before your feet do. A feet-together, knees-apart position can stress or strain your knee joints.

Move #46: Vertical Flutter Kicks

Equipment: Use flotation belt, vest, cuffs, or water jugs.

Starting Position: Move to water deep enough to bring your feet off the pool bottom. Bring your feet down so that your legs point straight downward. If your hands are free, circle them around each other in front of your chest.

Action: Flutter kick your legs from the hips in a short, brisk motion.

Variation: Vertical Flutter Spin: Rotate in a small circle as you flutter kick.

Move #47: Floating Mountain Climb

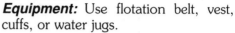

Equipment: Use flotation belt, vest, cuffs, or water jugs.

Starting Position: Move to water deep enough to bring your feet off the pool bottom. Bring your feet down so that your legs point straight downward.

Action:

1. Bring your right knee forward and up. Then extend the leg way out in front as if to hike up a steep incline. At the same time, press all the way back with the left leg. If your hands are free, simultaneously pump your arms, hands palm first against the water, in opposition to the movements of your legs.
2. Switch legs and repeat, alternating legs and arms, to cross the pool.

Work up to 16 repetitions.

Safety Tip: Maintain firmly contracted abdominal and buttocks muscles and a somewhat vertical torso position to protect your lower back.

Move #48: Bicycle Pump

Equipment: Use flotation belt, vest, cuffs, or water jugs.

Starting Position: Move to water deep enough to bring your feet off the pool bottom. Bring your feet down so that your legs point straight downward. Position your body so that you are "sitting" vertically.

Action: Contract your abdominal and buttocks muscles. Draw one knee toward your chest, no higher than hip height, while you extend the other leg toward the pool bottom. Switch legs.

Repeat the sequence briskly 16 times.

Variation: To increase intensity, increase surface area resistance by flexing your foot so that your ankle forms a right angle, rather than pointing your toes.

Move #49: Can-Can Soccer Kick

Equipment: Use flotation belt, vest, cuffs, or water jugs.

Starting Position: Move to water deep enough to bring your feet off the pool bottom. Imagine that you are sitting in a chair and adopt that position. Space your knees about 6 inches or 15 centimeters apart and bend both legs to 90 degrees. Firmly contract your abdominal and buttocks muscles.

Action:

1. Keep your feet and knees under the water and your hips stationary. Instead of kicking from the hips, extend your right leg from the knee, kicking your leg out straight.
2. Bend your right leg to 90 degrees. At the same time, kick out with your left leg.

Alternately kick and bend each leg for 16 repetitions.

Variation: To increase intensity by increasing surface area resistance, point your toes. For reduced intensity, flex your ankle.

AEROBIC COOL-DOWN

Use the same exercises as those described in "Warm-Up Aerobics" at the beginning of this chapter. Progressively reduce the range of motion, reduce traveling, and minimize jumping as you gradually lower the intensity of your aerobic exercises. Cool-down is an essential component of the aerobic exercise sequence that allows your body to adapt gradually to the decrease in cardiovascular demand. Skipping the cool-down can increase the chance of cardiovascular events or injuries at any age.

Advanced Conditioning Techniques

See Chapter 8 if you are interested in sampling the excitement of powerful peak aerobic plyometrics for cardiovascular fitness and neuromuscular power. Add advanced, explosive moves such as Plyometric Jacks and the Dolphin Jump when you are ready to obtain a higher level of fitness. Plyometrics employ powerful push-offs from the pool floor to raise your cardiovascular intensity and build balance and coordination skills.

CHAPTER

5

Water Exercises to Strengthen and Tone

M uscle stregthening and toning are important for more than aesthetic reasons. Studies show that regular, consistent exercise to improve and maintain muscular strength can prevent injuries and increase your chance of enjoying physical independence and mobility as you age. Exercises that incorporate high resistance for fewer repetitions increase strength *and* produce muscular endurance benefits, according to research completed in the 1980s. However, more repetitions at lower resistance seem to increase muscular endurance *without* necessarily increasing muscular strength.

Muscle strengthening and toning exercises also increase total lean body mass and improve the ratio of lean to fatty tissue. Therefore, as you develop a greater percentage of muscle tissue, your body metabolizes more calories at rest and while exercising. For that reason, muscle strengthening and toning should be a component of any weight management plan.

Muscle work in water increases muscle strength, endurance, and tone. If you wish to emphasize muscular strength over endurance, once you have mastered the basics, add resistance equipment such as that described in chapter 2. Perform each exercise in waist- to chest-deep water, and focus your attention on body position and your exertion on the muscles you are working. Each exercise instruction identifies the muscle group worked and explains equipment possibilities, body position, muscle action, proper breathing, and potential variations. Familiarize yourself with the following training definitions before you begin.

> *Contract*—Squeeze the muscle you are working to mobilize the muscle fibers into action.

> *Isolate*—Focus your energy on the muscle you are working, and minimize motion in the rest of your body.

> *Flex*—Decrease the angle between two ends of a joint, for example, by bending the knee.

> *Extend*—Increase the angle of the joint, for example, by straightening the elbow.

> *Abduct*—Move a limb away from the midline of the body.

> *Adduct*—Move a limb toward the midline of the body.

ABDOMINAL TECHNIQUES FOR FIRM RESULTS

The exercises that follow enable you to employ water's resistive qualities in the protective environment of aquatic bouyancy. Use the mental images described here to improve muscle and movement control, positioning, and breathing during this stimulating progression of highly effective abdominal exercises. Before you begin, familiarize yourself with the actual muscles you will be working (refer to Figure 2.6 on page 33) and focus your exertion on utilizing those muscles during each exercise. Then review the "Exercise Precautions" on pages 33 through 34.

Before you begin each abdominal exercise sequence, use this body awareness preparation to help you develop stronger abdominal control: Place your palms over the bottom half of both sides of your rib cage and contract the muscles over your rib cage. Use the imagery of closing an accordion or a fireplace bellows. Inhale and imagine that you can fill your abdominal cavity with air. Then contract your abdominals, the muscles above and below your navel and over your rib cage, and press your belly button toward your spine as you exhale. At the same time, contract your buttocks somewhat to brace your spine in the neutral position. Place your hands over your abdomen to feel the muscles contract.

Move #50: Standing Crunch

Equipment: Once you have mastered the basic exercise without equipment, add the use of a flotation belt, Body Buoys, or empty water jugs to increase flotation-oriented resistance.

Starting Position: Move to chest-deep water and put your back to the pool wall. Adopt the neutral position: feet shoulder-width apart, knees bent, abdominals firm, chest lifted, and shoulders back.

Action:

1. Identify the upper and lower ends of the *rectus abdominus* muscle—at the breastbone and just above the pelvis. Become aware of the muscles that surround the rib cage—the external and internal obliques.
2. Shorten the distance between the two ends of the abdominals, as though you were closing an accordion. Contract the muscles over your rib cage while you compress the abdominals and obliques toward the midline at the navel. Strive to bring the bottom of the ribs closer to your hip bones.
3. Release the contraction slowly.

Repeat the sequence 8 to 16 times.

Proper Breathing: Exhale on the contraction (close the accordion), inhale on the release. Refocus your attention on contracting the abdominal muscles while executing proper breathing.

Variations: Advanced fitness enthusiasts will be delighted with the results of performing the Standing Crunch with flotation equipment for resistance, a sequence that uses water's buoyancy to duplicate weight training effects. Plastic jugs, a flotation belt put on backwards with the strap in back and Body Buoys all provide good buoyancy resistance. You can reproduce the resistive qualities of a weight training machine by pressing against the flotation resistance of the buoys while contracting your abdominals for the Standing Crunch. Use one jug hugged to the chest at first, then two for additional resistance. Or hug the bubbles of your Body Buoys to your chest and perform the same exercise.

Walk to a depth where the jugs or buoys are slightly submerged. Hug the jug(s) to your body with your palms open and your fingertips over the tops of the jugs. Continue with the standing crunch sequence and note the increased muscle energy required to partially submerge the jugs using the strength of the abdominals. Then move the jugs to a position at the underarms (nestle the corner of the jug in the corner of your armpit) in order to focus on the muscles over and under the rib cage, the obliques. Increase the number of repetitions as you become more proficient. For variety, use a four-part count to move the body through abdominal contractions at four different ranges of motion, or hold contractions for four seconds and release.

If you use the reversed flotation belt, put both hands on top of the belt and perform the standing crunch. To focus on the muscles over your rib cage, put your left hand on the middle of your left thigh, your right hand on the top of the belt. Squeeze your abdominal muscles to bring your torso slightly forward and to the right. Continue for several repetitions. Repeat the sequence to the left.

Safety Tip: Avoid arching or hyperextending the lumbar spine during the release of the contraction. Check your alignment to be sure the position of your pelvis is appropriate. Your pelvis should be in a neutral position, not forward or backward, and braced firmly between an abdominal and buttocks contraction. Avoid a sitting motion because it defeats the purpose of the exercise. Give yourself a few weeks or months to master each progressively more challenging stage of this exercise.

Move #51: Floating Curl

Equipment: If you are using water jugs, hold them firmly under your arms. A flotation belt will enhance this exercise for beginning, intermediate, and advanced exercisers.

Starting Position: With flotation, lie back, extending the body so that you are floating face up on your back. Keep your knees slightly bent and avoid bringing your knees toward your chest.

Action:

1. Contract the abdominals while exhaling. Using the abdominal muscles, shorten the distance between your breastbone and your pelvis. If this is the first time you have performed this kind of exercise, you may not see any movement at all until your muscles get stronger.
2. Extend the body. Avoid arching your back each time you extend your body to a straightened position.

Proper Breathing: Exhale as you contract your abdominal muscles and inhale upon release.

Variation: The Oblique Floating Curl helps work the external and internal oblique muscles (the muscles on your sides and rib cage) and increases the water resistance against your abdominal muscles. Here's how to do it:

1. Place the sole of your left foot against your right thigh or shin. Bend your right leg.
2. Contract the muscles of your abdomen to bring the left side of your rib cage closer to your left hip bone. Try to avoid rolling your shoulders forward.

Repeat four to eight times, then switch the position to work the opposite side for four to eight repetitions. Over time, when your torso muscles feel stronger, gradually add more repetitions: Intersperse two or three sets of eight throughout your abdominal workout.

Safety Tip: Focus on the muscle energy of shortening the distance between breastbone and pelvis while contracting the abdominals to isolate the abdominal muscles.

Move #52: Sitting "V"

Equipment: If you are using water jugs, hold them firmly under your arms. A flotation belt will enhance this exercise for beginning, intermediate, and advanced exercisers.

Starting Position: With flotation, lie back, extending the body so that you are floating face up on your back.

Action:

1. Bring your legs out to the sides (open the "V"). At the same time, contract (squeeze) the abdominal muscles to bring your torso into a partially seated position, legs extended to either side.
2. Lie back, bring the legs together, and relax the abdominals.

Perform 8 to 16 repetitions.

Proper Breathing: Exhale as you contract your abdominal muscles and inhale upon release.

Variation: As you get stronger, add 16 more repetitions with a "double beat" at the fully abducted (open "V") and adducted (closed "V") positions. Use the added beat count to sustain a longer abdominal contraction.

Safety Tip: This exercise should be performed after you have mastered the other abdominal exercises and thereby strengthened your abdominals. If your adominals are weak, it is hard to escape the excessive arch of your lower back (anterior pelvic tilt and corresponding spinal hyperextension) that can cause back injury.

LOWER BODY STRENGTHENING AND TONING

Lower body exercises tone and strengthen the hips, thighs, buttocks, and lower legs (refer to figure 2.5 on page 32), producing a sleeker appearance and helping to prevent knee and back pain when performed properly. Concentrate on learning proper body position to enhance your results and prevent painful injuries associated with poor technique. If you focus on contracting the muscles indicated in the "muscle focus" for each exercise, you will achieve improvements more readily.

Advanced Conditioning Technique

Once you have mastered the lower body conditioning exercise in chapter 5, you can add power to your advanced workout. See "Powering Your Way to Fitness," beginning on page 158 in chapter 8 for some excellent advanced lower body toning Power Moves, such as Squat Step and Squat Knee Lift. You can employ Power Moves after your aerobic exercises to tone you up and cool you down while keeping your heart rate in the low end of your aerobic target zone.

Move #53: Outer/Inner Thigh Scissors

Equipment: If your torso and lower body muscles are basically strong, you may wish to wear resistance cuffs or boots on your lower legs or feet to increase intensity.

Muscle Focus: Exercises the muscles of the hip and the inner and outer thigh.

Starting Position: Perform this exercise in waist- to chest-deep water. Stand with your side to the wall and hold on to the pool deck with one hand for balance. Adopt the braced neutral position.

Action:

1. Lift your outside leg out to the side. Do not lean toward or away from the pool wall.
2. Contract the muscles of your inner thigh to bring your feet back together.

Repeat 8 to 16 times.

Change sides and repeat the exercise the same number of times with the other leg.

Variation: Scoop your outside palm in toward your body as you kick out. Then scoop your palm out to the side as you bring your feet back together. If you have a strong torso and no tendency toward lower back pain, vary your strength work by crossing in front of your stationary foot four times and in back of your foot four times.

Safety Tips: Keep your torso straight up and evenly balanced front to back and left to right. Lift only as high as you can without leaning to one side or moving your torso. Lift your leg only and avoid elevating your hip. Put your hand on your outside hip to help keep your hip stable. No motion should occur in the waist or neck. Pull in your abdominals and contract your buttocks to protect your lower back. Lift your chest and keep your shoulders back.

Move #54: Forward and Back Leg Glide

Equipment: If your torso and lower body muscles are strong, you may wish to wear resistance cuffs or boots on your lower legs or feet to increase intensity.

Muscle Focus: Exercises the muscles of the hip, buttocks, and front and back of the thigh.

Starting Position: Perform this exercise in waist- to chest-deep water. Stand with your side to the wall and hold on to the pool deck with one hand for balance. Squeeze the abdominals and buttocks to brace yourself in the neutral position.

Action:
1. Lift your *inside* leg forward from the hip to a comfortable height.
2. Reverse the direction of movement and press your leg backward only as far as you can without arching your lower back. Place your hand on your lower back to monitor your position.

Repeat the sequence 8 to 16 times. Turn around and repeat steps 1 and 2 with the other leg for the same number of repetitions.

Variations: Bend your knee or slow down the movement if you wish to decrease the intensity of this exercise. To add upper body activity, scoop your palm backward as you kick forward and scoop forward as you press your leg back.

Safety Tips: Pull in your abdominals firmly as you press your leg behind you. Keep your torso up straight. Limit the height of the backward kick to the point where you can maintain the position without arching your back. Higher is not better. No motion should occur in the torso, waist, or neck.

Move #55: Knee Kicks

Equipment: If your torso and lower body muscles are strong and you suffer no knee pain, you may wish to wear resistance cuffs or boots on your lower legs or feet to increase intensity.

Muscle Focus: Exercises the front and back of the thigh.

Starting Position: Perform this exercise in waist- to chest-deep water. Stand with your side to the wall and hold on to the pool deck with one hand for balance. Squeeze the abdominals and buttocks to brace yourself in the neutral position. Lift your inside leg to a right angle at hip and knee.

Action:
1. Contract the front of your thigh and kick your leg toward the pool's surface, pushing against water's resistance.
2. Then contract the back of your thigh and squeeze your buttocks to bend your knee.

Repeat 8 to 16 times. Turn around and repeat the same number of times with the other leg.

Variations: If you find it hard to hold your leg up, use the outside leg, reach behind your thigh and support your leg as you kick. Be sure to stand straight up with abdominals pulled in. Increase intensity by pointing the toes of your kicking leg. Reduce intensity by kicking with the foot flexed (put ankle at a right angle).

Safety Tips: Avoid locking your knee when you straighten your leg. Eliminate this exercise if you tend to experience knee pain, and add it to your routine when your knee is fully healed and pain free.

Move #56: Runner's Stride

Equipment: If your torso and lower body muscles are strong and you suffer no knee pain, you may wish to wear resistance cuffs or boots on your lower legs or feet to increase intensity.

Muscle Focus: Exercises the hip, buttocks, and the front and back of the thigh.

Starting Position: Perform this exercise in waist- to chest-deep water. Stand with your side to the wall and hold on to the pool deck with one hand for balance. Squeeze the abdominals and buttocks to brace yourself in the neutral position.

Action:
1. Lift your inside leg to a right angle at hip and knee.
2. Kick your foot toward the surface.
3. Press your straight leg down and back behind you.
4. Kick your heel toward your buttocks.

Repeat the full sequence 8 to 16 times. Turn around and repeat the same number of times with the other leg.

Safety Tips: Focus on maintaining a strongly supported neutral position without leaning forward or back or arching your lower back. Eliminate this exercise if you tend to experience knee pain and add it to your routine when your knee is fully healed and pain free.

Move #57: Hip Side Press

Equipment: If your torso and lower body muscles are strong and you suffer no hip pain, you may wish to wear resistance cuffs or boots on your lower legs or feet to increase intensity.

Muscle Focus: Exercises the hip and buttocks.

Starting Position: Perform this exercise in waist- to chest-deep water. Stand with your side to the wall and hold on to the pool deck with one hand for balance. Squeeze the abdominals and buttocks to brace yourself in the neutral position. Lift your outside leg to a right angle at hip and knee.

Action:

1. Press your knee out toward the pool wall.
2. Press your knee back to the starting position.

Repeat 8 to 16 times. Turn around and repeat the same number of times with the other leg.

Variation: Help improve lower body alignment by performing a smooth motion: Lift your knee, press it out toward the wall, then bring it back to the starting position and put your foot down. Repeat the exercise 8 to 16 times on each side.

Safety Tips: Protect your hip and back by moving slowly and with control. Avoid turning your torso: Place your hand on your abdomen to make sure you are not twisting your torso as you press your knee out and in. To protect your knee joint, avoid bending your knee beyond 90 degrees.

Move #58: Pivoted Dips

Muscle Focus: Exercises the buttocks and the front and back of the thigh.

Starting Position: Perform this exercise in waist-deep water. Stand with your side to the wall and hold on to the pool deck with one hand for balance. Squeeze the abdominals and buttocks to brace yourself in the neutral position. Place one leg behind the other and stretch your outside arm out to your side, palm facing down.

Action:

1. Lower your back knee toward the pool floor as you press your outside palm down to your side.
2. Press yourself back up using the front leg as you lift your arm, palm up, out to the side.

Repeat eight times, pivot turn on your toes to switch sides, and repeat eight times.

Variation: Perform this exercise with your hand on your hip if you find it difficult to coordinate your arms.

Safety Tip: Be sure your front knee is positioned over your heel, not pushed forward over your toes.

Move #59: Supported Squats

Muscle Focus: Exercises the hip, buttocks, and the front and back of the thigh. Helps build strong knee support.

Starting Position: Perform this exercise in waist-deep water. Stand facing the wall or ladder and hold on with both hands. Bring your feet shoulder-width or hip-width apart, knees pointing the same direction as your first and second toes. Squeeze the abdominals and buttocks to brace yourself in the neutral position.

Action:

1. Lift your chest and push your buttocks back and down as if you are lowering yourself toward a chair placed a foot or 30 centimeters or so behind you. Squat to about 1/3 of the way toward the imaginary chair.

2. Press through your feet to come back to a standing, upright position.

Perform 8 to 16 repetitions.

Variation: Bring your feet further apart and turn them out slightly. Complete 8 to 10 repetitions.

Safety Tips: Contract your abdominal muscles firmly and avoid arching your back.

Move #60: Calf Lifts

Muscle Focus: Exercises the back of the calf.

Starting Position: Perform this exercise in waist- to chest-deep water. Face the pool deck and hold on to the edge. Stand up straight an arm's length from the pool wall with feet shoulder-width apart and knees relaxed. Contract the abdominals and buttocks to brace yourself in the neutral position.

Action:

1. Raise yourself up onto your toes.
2. Slowly lower your heels to the floor.

Repeat 8 to 16 times.

Variation: Bring your feet farther apart and turn them out slightly. Complete 8 to 10 repetitions.

Move #61: Toe Lifts

Muscle Focus: Exercises the shins.

Starting Position: Perform this exercise in waist- to chest-deep water. Face the pool deck and hold on to the edge. Stand up straight an arm's length from the pool wall with feet wider than shoulder-width apart and knees flexed and relaxed. Squeeze the abdominals and buttocks to brace yourself in the neutral position. Point your feet out slightly to the sides.

Action:

1. Lift your toes, keeping your heels on the floor.
2. Press your toes back toward the floor.

Repeat 16 times.

Variation: Lift one foot at a time, tapping twice on one side and twice on the other. Repeat eight times.

UPPER BODY STRENGTHENING AND TONING

Good upper body strength makes performing daily chores easier and helps prevent injuries. The upper body exercises work the chest, back, shoulders, and upper arms. Review Figure 2.8 on page 35 to familiarize yourself with the location of the muscles you will use. Try these exercises without equipment the first time. Then, if you have no upper body joint problems, add webbed gloves, disks, kick boards, or water bells for added strength and toning. Remember to establish a solid level of strength before adding new resistance to your routine. To do otherwise may cause injury.

Here's how to use disks: Get into your starting position and hold the disks up out of the water on the palms of your hands, waiter style. Put the disks in the water and immediately begin your desired movement. Keep pressure against the disks at all times to keep them in position.

Move #62: Chest/Upper Back Glide

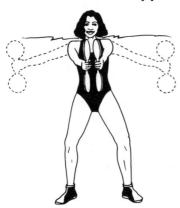

Equipment: Use disks, webbed gloves, water exercise bells, or paddles.

Muscle Focus: Exercises the chest and upper back.

Starting Position: Perform this exercise in chest- to shoulder-deep water. Stand with one foot in front of the other and a comfortable and stable distance apart. Contract the abdominals and buttocks to brace yourself in the neutral position. Your shoulders should be partly submerged.

Action:

1. Extend both arms out to sides, palms facing forward.
2. Press both palms in toward one another out in front of your chest.
3. Turn your palms around and press back until your hands are even with your back.

Turn your palms around and repeat the sequence for 8 to 16 repetitions.

Variation: To change direction while using disks, turn your palms around before they meet at the center. Turn you hands over again as soon as your arms are even with your back and press them immediately toward the center.

Safety Tip: For greater stability, perform one arm at a time, holding on to the pool edge with your side toward the wall.

Move #63: Chest/Back Press

Equipment: Use disks, webbed gloves, a small kick board, water exercise bells, or paddles.

Muscle Focus: Exercises the chest and mid back.

Starting Position: Perform this exercise in chest- to shoulder-deep water. Stand with one foot in front of the other and a comfortable and stable distance apart. Contract the abdominals and buttocks to brace yourself in the neutral position. Your shoulders should be partly submerged.

Action:
1. Press the disk, board, or your hands out in front of your chest, under water. Contract the muscles over your shoulder blades and keep them contracted during the entire exercise.
2. Pull the disk, board, or your hands back toward your rib cage, bringing your elbows along your sides to a comfortable point behind your waist. Use the muscles of your mid back.

Repeat 8 to 16 times.

Variations: If you are using disks, grasp one disk (or put two plates together) and hold on to the outer edges. If you are using equipment other than disks or kick boards, try performing with the elbows elevated out to your sides, but stop the pull back motion before your elbows move behind your back.

Safety Tips: When you straighten your arms, keep a slight bend at the elbow to protect the elbow joint. Hold your abdominals firmly to stabilize your torso. For greater stability, perform one arm at a time, holding on to the pool edge, your side toward the wall.

Move #64: Diagonal Front Shoulder Press

Equipment: Use webbed gloves, water exercise bells, or paddles.

Muscle Focus: Exercises the muscles of the shoulder's rotator cuff.

Starting Position: Perform this exercise in shoulder-deep water. Stand with your left side next to the wall and hold on to the pool edge with your left hand for stability. Place your left (inside) foot back, your right (outside) foot forward, a comfortable distance apart. Contract the abdominals and buttocks to brace yourself in the neutral position. Your shoulders should be partly submerged. Reach out in front of your right leg with your right hand, palm down.

Action:

1. Press your right palm down and across your body toward your left thigh.
2. Lift your arm up toward the pool surface to return to the starting position.

Repeat eight times. Then switch your position with a pivot turn and repeat eight times.

Move #65: Pivoted Shoulder Press

Equipment: Use webbed gloves, disks, water exercise bells, or paddles.

Muscle Focus: Exercises the front and back of the shoulder.

Starting Position: Perform this exercise in chest- to shoulder-deep water. Stand with one foot in front of the other and a comfortable and stable distance apart. Contract your abdominals and buttocks to brace yourself in the neutral position and stabilize your torso. Bring both arms behind you. Your shoulders should be partly submerged.

Action:

1. Press both palms forward and toward the pool surface, out in front of your chest.
2. Turn your hands around and press your palms down past your sides, behind your hips.

Repeat 8 to 16 times.

Safety Tips: Keep your shoulders down and back and as you press back, stop at the point of comfortable resistance. Keep your hands under water during the entire exercise. For greater stability, perform one arm at a time, holding on to the pool edge, your side toward the wall.

Move #66: Side Arm Pump

Equipment: Use webbed gloves, disks, water exercise bells, or paddles.

Muscle Focus: Exercises the top and outside of the shoulder and the side of your torso, under your arm.

Starting Position: Perform this exercise in chest- to shoulder-deep water. Stand with one foot in front of the other and a comfortable and stable distance apart. Keep your arms at your sides and contract your abdominals and buttocks to brace yourself in the neutral position and stabilize your torso.

Action:

1. Slowly lift both arms out to your sides, palms up, toward the water's surface.
2. Slowly press both arms down to your sides, palms down.

Repeat 8 to 16 times.

Variation: Lift both arms out to your sides, then press them down behind your buttocks instead of to your sides. Imagine that you are squeezing a beach ball behind your back.

Safety Tips: Keep your hands under water throughout the entire exercise. For greater stability, perform one arm at a time, holding on to the pool edge with your side toward the pool wall. Minimize this exercise by reducing speed and repetitions if you have neck pain.

Move #67: Upper Arm Curls

Equipment: Use webbed gloves, disks, water exercise bells, or paddles.

Muscle Focus: Exercises the front and back of the upper arm.

Starting Position: Perform this exercise in chest- to shoulder-deep water. Stand with one foot in front of the other and a comfortable and stable distance apart. Pull in your abdominals and buttocks to brace yourself in the neutral position and stabilize your torso. Bring both arms behind you, palms facing forward. Keep your elbows behind your waist for this exercise.

Action:
1. Bend your elbows. Keeping your upper arms motionless, press your palms upward toward the surface of the pool in an arc. Avoid lifting your hands out of the water.
2. Turn your palms toward the pool bottom and press down and back.

Repeat 8 to 16 times.

Safety Tips: Keep a slight bend in the elbow when you extend to protect the elbow joint. If you are using water exercise bells or paddles, you will not need to turn your hand around between Steps 1 and 2. For greater stability, perform poolside, one arm at a time, holding on to the pool edge.

Move #68: Traffic Cop

Equipment: Use webbed gloves, disks, water exercise bells, or paddles.

Muscle Focus: Exercises the muscles of the shoulder's rotator cuff. Helps correct and prevent rounded shoulders.

Starting Position: Perform this exercise in chest- to shoulder-deep water. Stand with one foot in front of the other or shoulder-width apart and a comfortable and stable distance apart. Pull in your abdominals and buttocks to brace yourself in the neutral position and stabilize your torso. Bring both arms behind you, palms facing forward. Keep your elbows behind your waist. Nestle your elbows into your waist. Imagine that your upper arms are velcroed to your sides and leave them in that position throughout the exercise. Your shoulders should be partly submerged.

Action:

1. Without moving your upper arms, press both hands to the right in an arc. Keep your elbows snugly positioned at your waist and avoid twisting your torso.
2. Press both hands to the left.

Repeat 8 to 16 times.

Variation: If you are using bells or paddles, perform this exercise using the wall for stability with your back against the pool wall.

Safety Tip: For greater stability, perform one arm at a time, holding on to the pool edge, your side toward the wall.

Move #69: Shoulder Shrugs and Rolls

Equipment: Use water exercise bells or paddles.

Muscle Focus: Exercises the upper back and shoulder muscles.

Starting Position: Perform this exercise in chest- to shoulder-deep water. Stand with feet shoulder-width apart, arms at your sides. Pull in your abdominals and buttocks to brace yourself in the neutral position and stabilize your torso. Bring both arms behind you, palms facing forward.

Action:

1. Shrug your shoulders slowly by bringing them up toward your ears.
2. Slowly press your shoulders down.
   Repeat eight times.
3. Roll your shoulders forward, up, back, and down.
   Repeat eight times.

Move #70: Behind-the-Back Press

Equipment: Use one disk, one bell, one paddle, or webbed gloves.

Muscle Focus: Exercises the upper back and shoulder muscles.

Starting Position: Perform this exercise in chest- to shoulder-deep water. Stand with feet shoulder-width apart, arms at your sides. Pull in your abdominals and buttocks to brace yourself in the neutral position and stabilize your torso. Bring both hands behind you, palms facing upward, or holding the equipment.

Action:

1. Keeping your hands behind you, bend your elbows and lift your hands upward toward your waist.
2. Press your hands back down.

Repeat eight times.

Variation: To add resistance, bring your hands behind you and grasp either side of the disk, bell, or paddle, holding its flat surface parallel to the pool floor. Perform the exercise as described.

Move #71: Cat Back Press

Muscle Focus: Exercises the back muscles.

Starting Position: Place your feet more than shoulder-width apart, toes pointed slightly out to either side. Bend your knees and pull in your abdominals. Put your hands on your thighs midway between your knees and your hips.

Action:

1. Contract your abdomen and buttocks and press the middle of your back up toward the sky like a cat stretching its back.
2. Flatten your back so that it is parallel to the pool floor.

Repeat 8 to 16 times.

Final Cool-Down

Flexibility exercises are an important part of any exercise program. Good flexibility has been shown to decrease the incidence of many types of injuries. For example, chronic lower back pain often arises due to weakened abdominal muscles and inadequate flexibility in the muscles of the lower back, back of the thigh, and calf.

Your flexibility is a product of your heredity and exercise and may vary from one part of your body to another. Cooling your muscles in their lengthened position after exercise will help keep your muscles from becoming shortened, stiff, and sore. Effective stretch techniques can make or break the success of your flexibility endeavors. For instance, research suggests that you can make better and safer progress by stretching muscles when they are warm. If you prefer, you can stretch a specific muscle group immediately after you have worked it during the strengthening and toning section. However, putting your stretch routine at the end of your program can also help you relax and reduce stress because it allows your body to return gradually to a resting state.

Be careful not to overdo flexibility training. Avoid pushing too hard, holding positions too long, or using positions that cause pain. Stretch three to five times per week as part of your regular exercise routine.

Some people benefit from warming up and stretching *every* day. When you begin your workout, warm your muscles with slow, rhythmic exercise performed through a moderate range of motion before stretching. Water enhances the range of motion and pain-free mobility needed for adequate flexibility training. However, some commonly employed stretching exercises can increase your risk of musculoskeletal injuries. Carefully follow the guidelines suggested in the stretch diagrams illustrated in chapter 3 and in this chapter to minimize the chance of injury.

COOL-DOWN STRETCH SEQUENCE

Perform all of the stretches you did during warm-up, but hold each static stretch for about twice as long (20 to 30 seconds). Remember, stretching should never be painful; stretch only to the point of comfortable resistance. Double check your position or eliminate the stretch for the time being if it causes you discomfort. If you feel cool because you are standing relatively motionless in water, you may continuously move the limbs that are not involved in the stretch to keep warm.

The flexibility exercises illustrated in chapter 3 provide a quick reference for all the stretches you need for an effective Cool-Down Stretch sequence. See pages 59 to 69 if you would like to review specific stretch instructions for each position.

COOL-DOWN STRETCH SUPPLEMENT

Now add these neck, shoulder, and upper back stretches to improve flexibility in areas that often become tense.

Move #72: Safe Neck Stretch

Starting Position: Stand with feet shoulder-width apart in the braced neutral position.

Action 1: Reach behind your back and bring your right arm toward your left hip. Gently grasp your right wrist with your left hand. Slowly lower your left ear toward your left shoulder. Hold for 20 to 30 seconds, then return your head to an upright position. Repeat the stretch on the opposite side.

Action 2: Reach behind your back and bring your right arm toward your left hip. Gently grasp your right wrist with your left hand. Slowly turn your head so that you are looking toward your left shoulder. Hold for 20 to 30 seconds, then turn your head slowly forward. Repeat the stretch for the opposite side.

Safety Tips: Remember to stretch *only to the point of comfortable resistance*. If you feel pulling or pain, you are stretching too far. Slowly reduce the amount of stretch. Move *very slowly* from one position to the next, or you will be injured.

Move #73: Shoulder Hug

Starting Position: Stand with feet shoulder-width apart in the braced neutral position.

Action: Reach both hands across your chest and back toward your shoulder blades. Relax your upper back while you hold the stretch for 10 to 15 seconds. Switch arms, putting the other arm on top.

PART
III

Designing Your Special Water Workout

The key to achieving good fitness is to find and maintain a program that is right for you. Like buying shoes, "one size fits all" just doesn't work when it comes to fitness. To find a workout program that fits well, and to stick with it, you need to learn how to identify your own, individual fitness needs and objectives and how to achieve them. In chapter 7, you can learn about your particular body type and how it affects your workout choices; address special concerns such as arthritis, cardiac recovery, or injury recovery; or choose the right exercises if you are pregnant or an older adult. In Chapter 8, discover ways to intensify your workout with advanced power and plyometric techniques. Each section provides clear instructions for planning your personal water workout program based on what's best for you.

CHAPTER

7

Creating Your Fitness Plan

Enhance your fitness success by creating a fitness plan that is right for your needs and circumstances and by making a commitment to yourself to fit water exercise into your life. If you identify your objectives, make a plan for meeting those goals, build a new habit one step at a time, approach obstacles with creativity and enthusiasm, and reward yourself for making progress, you will nearly guarantee your success. If you are comfortable with keeping records, a personal fitness journal will help you clearly identify your path and track your achievements. First identify your goals and methods by using the information in this chapter, particularly the segments on "Workouts for Specific Body Types," pages 124 through 126, and "Water Workouts for Special Concerns," pages 127 through 156, and chapter 8, "Intensifying Your Workout," page 157. If you like, you can use weekly and monthly diaries to track your results, overcome barriers, and reward yourself. If you prefer not to use a written plan, simply choose the water workout sequence that seems best for you and aim to exercise once every other day. As you build new fitness habits, remember the wise words spoken by wellness professional Murray Banks of Peak Performance: "Inch by inch it's a cinch. . . . Yard by yard it's too hard." If you are patient but persistent, and change just a little bit at a time, your efforts will be rewarded with success.

If you understand the basic principles that affect your body's ability to become more fit, you'll be able to make sound decisions when devising and implementing your fitness plan. The fitness principles that follow provide a simple and fundamental tool for improving your level of fitness.

FITNESS PRINCIPLES

You can make yourself more fit by using the **overload principle**. The muscles, including the heart, will get stronger if you gradually place greater demands on them than they are used to performing. If you stretch a muscle a little longer or more often than it is used to being stretched, it will become more flexible. If you exercise a bit longer or more intensely than you are accustomed to exercising, your muscular or cardiovascular endurance will increase. *Overuse* occurs if you take the overload principle too far.

Exercise specificity means that you must perform an exercise activity that specifically works the fitness component, body system, and muscles you want to fortify. For example, you must perform aerobic exercise activity to strengthen the aerobic energy system, burn fat, or increase the endurance of the cardiovascular system, or hamstring flexibility exercises to increase the flexibility of your hamstrings. When overloading the abdominal muscles to increase their strength, you will not necessarily see any benefit to the cardiovascular system in the form of increased aerobic fitness.

The **reversibility principle** says that your fitness level will gradually decline if you become inactive. If the strengthened system, muscle, or organ is not exercised sufficiently and regularly, your fitness adaptations will be lost. In other words, use it or lose it. If you skip a few days or weeks of your workout, don't worry; you can eventually return to your original program, but it is important to start back very gradually. Trying to get right back into it at the level you exercised before you took a break can, and often does, produce injuries.

TAILORED SEQUENCES

Tailored sequences allow you to come to terms with the fact that every person has different exercise needs and objectives. Follow the guidelines suggested here to help you choose and follow the best program for you.

Each segment lists exercises and directions appropriate to the specific situation. Remember to consult your doctor first if there is any question about your readiness to begin an exercise program.

Your First Water Workout

Your first water workout will show you how comfortable, satisfying, and invigorating exercise can be. The primary objective is to become familiar with how your body moves in the water and how you can control your movements with a bit of practice and concentration. As you continue to pursue aqua fitness regularly, adapting to the special balance and agility aspects of the aquatic environment will become second nature for you. You will be able to judge how long to continue exercising by how you feel. During the aerobic and muscle toning segments, you'll know it's time to change what you are doing when you feel fatigue coming on. During your aerobic section, fatigue is a signal for you to begin the gradual descent of an aerobic cool-down. During muscle toning, fatigue indicates that it's time to change to another exercise. If you are still charged up after eight repetitions, complete about eight more, but never continue to exercise once you feel fatigue. To do so greatly increases your risk of injury or illness.

There is absolutely no need to push yourself when you begin any new exercise program. Your body must adapt gradually to the introduction of exercise. So take it easy the first several times you work out. Get to know your muscles and how they work together to move your joints and stabilize your body: Develop "body awareness." When you become adept at controlling your muscle movements and breathing, you can begin to intensify your program along the FIT (frequency, intensity, and time) principle. Increase very gradually in *one category at a time*, and allow several weeks between each type of increase for your body to adapt to the new challenge. For instance, if your aerobic section is 10 minutes long, increase it to 11 minutes the next week, 12 minutes the following week, and so on until you reach your objective. If you are exercising three times a week and wish to add a day, exercise four times a week for a shorter period each time for several weeks, then gradually increase the duration. If you plan to increase muscle strengthening intensity with equipment, start out with no equipment until you are steady and strong in your water resistance exercises. Then build your intensity gradually, by adding equipment and increasing the force or speed of your movements.

Before you begin your first water workout, check with your doctor to find out if you need medical clearance before beginning exercise. Next, consult the "Water Workouts for Special Concerns" section of this chapter starting on page 127 to learn how to address any particular considerations important to you. Then reread the "Injury Prevention Checklist" on pages 21 through 25. Check to make sure your pool is about 78 to 86 degrees Fahrenheit or 26 to 30 degrees centigrade and that someone is nearby in case you need assistance. Table 7.1 provides an introductory water workout sequence. Follow it the first several times you work out in the pool, tailoring it to your changing needs as you improve your fitness. Refer to the descriptions in Part II for more detailed instructions on each exercise.

Table 7.1
Your First Water Workout

(35 to 45 minutes)

Follow this sequence the first several times you work out in the pool. Before you start, familiarize yourself with the specific instructions for each exercise and stretch provided in Part II.

Thermal Warm-Up (5 minutes)	Perform this Thermal Warm-Up sequence twice. Start slowly and build very gradually.
	Move #1 Water Walk: 30 seconds
	Move #2 Pedal Jog: 30 seconds
	Move #9 Heel Jacks: 8 times
	Move #10 Alternate Leg Press Backs: 8 times
	Move #29 Snake Walk: 1 minute
Warm-Up Stretch (5 minutes)	Hold each stretch position for 10 seconds.
	Move #12 Outer Thigh Stretch
	Move #13 Lower Back Stretch With Ankle Rotation
	Move #14 Front of Thigh Stretch
	Move #15 Shin Stretch and Shoulder Shrug
	Move #16 Inner Thigh Step Out
	Move #17 Hip Flexor Stretch
	Move #18 Straight Leg Calf Stretch
	Move #19 Bent Knee Calf Stretch
	Move #20 Hamstring Stretch
	(Repeat previous sequence for other side of body.)
	Move #21 Deep Muscle Buttocks Stretch
	Move #22 Full Back Stretch
	Move #23 Mid-Back Stretch

	Move #24	Elbow Press Back
	Move #25	Chest Stretch with Shoulder Rolls
	Move #26	Upper Back Stretch
	Move #27	Torso and Shoulder Stretch
	Move #28	Shoulder and Upper Arm Stretch

Aerobic Exercises
(10-15 minutes)

In this section, start slowly, build gradually, then gradually decrease intensity.

Move #1	Water Walk: 1 minute
Move #2	Pedal Jog: 30 seconds
Move #9	Heel Jacks: 8 times
Move #10	Alternate Leg Press Backs: 8 times
Move #30	Step Wide Side: 8 times each direction
Move #31	Hydro Jacks: 8 times
Move #32	Cross-Country Ski: 16 times
Move #29	Snake Walk: 1 minute
Move #42	Aqua Ski: 10-30 seconds
Move #43	Floating Side Scissors: 10-30 seconds
Move #44	Back Float Kick and Squiggle: 10-30 seconds
Move #46	Vertical Flutter Kicks: 10-30 seconds
Move #48	Bicycle Pump: 10-30 seconds
Move #29	Snake Walk: 1 minute
Move #30	Step Wide Side: 8 times right, 8 times left
Move #10	Alternate Leg Press Backs: 8 times
Move #9	Heel Jacks: 8 times
Move #1	Water Walk: 1 minute
Move #2	Pedal Jog: 30 seconds

Muscle Strengthening
and Toning Exercises
(5-10 minutes)

Move #50	Standing Crunch: 8 times
Move #51	Floating Curl: 8 times
Move #53	Outer/Inner Thigh Scissors: 8 times
Move #54	Forward and Back Leg Glide: 8 times per side
Move #58	Pivoted Dips: 4 times per side
Move #60	Calf Lifts: 8 times
Move #61	Toe Lifts: 8 times per foot
Move #62	Chest/Upper Back Glide: 8 times

(continued)

Table 7.1   (*continued*)

Muscle Strengthening and Toning Exercises (*continued*)	Move #65	Pivoted Shoulder Press: 8 times
	Move #66	Side Arm Pump: 4 times
	Move #67	Upper Arm Curls: 8 times
	Move #69	Shoulder Shrugs and Rolls: 4 times each
Final Cool-Down Stretches (10 minutes)	Repeat the entire Warm-Up Stretch sequence, but hold each stretch for 20 seconds. Add the following Final Cool-Down Stretches:	
	Move #72 Safe Neck Stretch	
	Move #73 Shoulder Hug	

Workouts for Specific Body Types

Have you ever wondered why some people seem to become slim and toned after just a few weeks of exercise, while others have to follow the identical exercise and nutrition practices for many months to achieve similar results? Is everyone potentially a slender model or muscular body builder? No, and here's why.

There are three main hereditary body types: ectomorph, endomorph, and mesomorph (see Figure 7.1). Most people generally fit into one category or another, or have traits of two types mixed together. If you're unsure of your body type, identify the traits you had as a teenager, before your lifestyle may have disguised your true genetic characteristics.

Ectomorphs tend to be long and lanky. They are small-boned, with limbs longer in relation to the trunk. Muscles are not well defined. Ectomorphs are not likely to increase much in muscle size or bulk but have an easier time with weight control because of their faster metabolisms.

Endomorphs are rounded and soft. The body tends to be pear-shaped, with soft, rounded shoulders and wider, padded hips. Limbs are shorter relative to the trunk. Endomorphs often have slower metabolisms.

The hourglass-shaped mesomorph builds muscle easily. Mesomorphs are broader at the shoulders and hips, narrower at the waist. Their well-developed and defined muscles make them look fit even if they don't exercise. Their lack of flexibility can expose them to the risk of upper back, neck, and lower leg injury.

Many people display combinations of body types. "Endo-meso-morphs" have well-defined muscles and higher ratios of fat and tend to carry more weight in the hips and thighs. "Ecto-mesomorphs" are long, thin, and wiry, with well-defined muscles. "Endo-ectomorphs" tend to

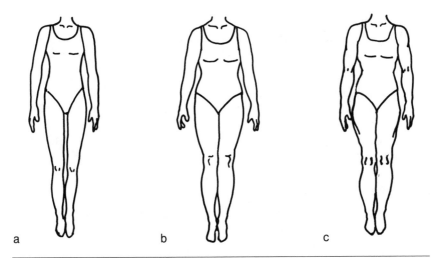

Figure 7.1   The ectomorph (a), endomorph (b), and mesomorph (c).

carry more weight in the hips and thighs, although they are long-limbed and small-boned. They must work harder to tone muscle and to control accumulation of fat storage.

Each body type has advantages and disadvantages. The point is to identify your own characteristics and develop realistic and appropriate fitness objectives. You will look and feel your best when you are healthy and fit. Choose an exercise plan based on your own characteristics and your personal fitness objectives.

Exercise for the Ectomorphic Body

Follow the Basic Water Workout program, but focus on muscle toning. Gradually add increased resistance by using water equipment described in chapter 2. Emphasize strengthening exercises for the abdominals and trunk to prevent lower back problems.

Exercise Objectives and Results.   The ectomorph's muscles get somewhat stronger with conditioning but require more effort and time to appear firm and toned. A thin body can still be proportionally high in body fat (overfat), so ectomorphs need to pursue aerobic training to maintain good health. Gradually strengthen the abdominals and trunk and work carefully on torso and lower-body flexibility to combat susceptibility to lower back problems.

Exercise for the Endomorphic Body

You can improve your body composition and speed up your metabolism by following the basic water workout program and concentrating on the weight control recommendations described in "Toning Up and Losing Weight" on this page. Endomorphs can be prone to injury from impact stress. It is essential that you protect your joints through low impact exercise, so water exercise is a method of choice.

Exercise Objectives and Results. Body toning and weight control can be more challenging for this genetic body type because of higher fat to lean tissue ratios (body composition). Aerobic conditioning and resistance or weight training can improve body composition, metabolism, and muscle definition.

Exercise for the Mesomorphic Body

Mesomorphs frequenty have taut, firm muscles. Tense muscles lead to pain and discomfort and can limit your mobility, especially later in life. Lengthen the final stretch/flexibility section of your routine to 10 or 15 minutes to relax tight muscles. You should work on improved aerobic endurance for functional stamina and cardiovascular health because mesomorphs can be prone to heart and circulatory ailments. So strive for three water workouts each week that include a full aerobics section and that conclude with a relaxing flexibility segment. You may want to further develop your naturally muscular physique by gradually increasing the resistance used during Muscle Strengthening and Toning exercises.

Exercise Objectives and Results. Mesomorphs respond quickly to resistance training and become firm and toned with less effort than ectomorphs or endomorphs. The mesomorphic body type is quick to drop fat but usually needs to work on flexibility to relax tight muscles and on aerobic conditioning to improve cardiovascular endurance and stamina. Because mesomorphs look fit even if they are out of shape, some may be less motivated to exercise. Mesomorphs tend to add weight in the abdomen if they neglect the need to exercise.

Toning Up and Losing Weight

Remember, you must burn off excess fat aerobically. To focus your efforts on weight control, increase your lean body mass and reduce the fat mass. In other words, build the duration and intensity of your aerobic exercise gradually over a period of several months and increase your muscle resistance training gradually.

Aerobic endurance activities can train your body to become a more efficient fat burner. Muscle strengthening can build your lean tissue mass. Unlike fatty tissue, lean tissue burns calories even when you are at rest. So include muscle strength and endurance exercises not only to tone up, but also to increase the rate at which you burn calories all the time.

To see progress, you must exercise every other day, or three times a week. Build up to five days each week as you increase your fitness level. To change your body composition by increasing lean tissue, two of your five workouts should focus on strengthening and toning exercises. If you are just getting back in shape and want to encourage greater fat burning, gradually lengthen the duration of your aerobic activity rather than push for the highest possible intensity. High intensity aerobic activity often brings on fatigue faster and produces injuries unless you are extremely fit.

For the best results, combine your exercise program with a healthy eating plan. Always eat breakfast, gradually reduce your intake of empty calories from fats and simple sugars (cut no more than 500 calories from your daily intake), and drink lots of fluids, especially water.

WATER WORKOUTS FOR SPECIAL CONCERNS

The same water properties that make water exercise an excellent workout option for almost everyone also prove true for people with special health concerns and objectives. Experience has shown that appropriate water exercise can notably enhance the recovery, health, and well-being of individuals in cardiac recovery, pregnant women, people with arthritis, older adults, and those rehabilitating from injuries and movement limitations. Discuss your concerns and plan your specialized water workout program with a qualified health professional before you proceed. Use the guidelines in the remainder of this chapter to help you tailor your program to your own health needs.

Cardiac Recovery

People at risk of cardiac disturbance require longer warm-up and more gradual cool-down periods. Cardiac rehabilitation professionals strongly recommend that you train aerobically three to five days each week. It may be necessary to lower the intensity and duration of your aerobic training, in which case you will need to exercise four to six times per week and eventually increase the duration of your workouts.

To promote injury-free functioning, your workout should include strength training and flexibility work as well as aerobic/cardiovascular exercise. Focus on breathing fully throughout your workout. Use "belly breathing," in which you expand your whole belly when you breath, rather than involving just your ribs and chest. To help develop your ability to belly breathe, practice pushing your belly against your waistband when you exhale. Strive to breathe in an even rhythm. (Research suggests that the most efficient breathing rate during vigorous aerobic exercise is about 30 breaths per minute.) While no exercises in this book include exertions that require holding your breath, known as the Valsalva maneuver, it bears mentioning that you must avoid any tendency to hold your breath, especially when holding a squeezed or contracted muscle, and stay away from activities such as isometrics, holding up heavy objects, or pressing against a wall. While contracting a muscle to work on muscle strength, use "straw breathing:" Inhale deeply, then blow out through pursed lips as you squeeze the muscle firmly.

Experts agree that a well-rounded cardiac recovery program (including cardiovascular conditioning, strength training, and flexibility exercises) as soon as possible after surgery can help prepare patients to return to work and leisure activities. The basic components of a training session for people in cardiac recovery appear in Table 7.2. Noted cardiac rehabilitation researchers Pollock, Wilmore, and Fox suggest that the first six to eight weeks of your recovery exercise program should be monitored by cardiac medical professionals.

Table 7.2
Basic Components of a Cardiac Training Session

Component	Duration
Thermal Warm-Up	10 minutes
Warm-Up Stretch	10 minutes
Muscular Conditioning	10 minutes
Aerobic Exercise (mild intensity with very gradual warm-up and very gradual cool-down)	5 to 60 minutes
Cool-Down (stretch for flexibility)	5 to 10 minutes

Qualified health professionals can determine if there are health factors that would require exercise restrictions. They can devise the right exercise program for your health situation and keep track of your exercise responses to be sure you are on the right program.

Cardiac Recovery Workout

Cardiologists and researchers at the University of Rhode Island Human Performance Lab have revealed valuable information regarding water's thermal qualities, adjustable intensity, and improved dynamics for cardiovascular fitness. Their carefully monitored scientific studies of water-versus land-based exercise unveiled previously undocumented factors that may make water exercise a superior avenue for cardiac rehabilitation exercise.

Water-based exercise was shown to produce a lower incidence of arrhythmias, or irregular heartbeat, which can signal cardiac disturbances. The mitigating factor here is water temperature. As a result of their findings, University of Rhode Island researchers recommend exercising in water at what they call "thermoneutral temperature." During vertical aerobic exercise, thermoneutral water temperature is usually 83 to 86 degrees Fahrenheit or 28 to 30 degrees centigrade.

Cardiac arrest and other major cardiovascular events are not common in cardiac rehabilitation programs. The best way to handle potential emergency situations is to exercise under qualified supervision. To prevent medical emergencies, your health professional will help you monitor your heart rate, blood pressure, and work intensity, and guide you through the progressive phases of recovery. Once you have progressed beyond the three medically established phases of recovery, you can continue your water workout program on your own and check in periodically for evaluation. Be sure to return for professional exercise evaluation whenever you change your exercise routine.

Before you begin your workout, check the pool temperature to be sure it is between 83 and 86 degrees Fahrenheit or 28 to 30 degrees centigrade. Then, follow the Cardiac Recovery Workout sequence in Table 7.3. Start out with very moderate intensity levels and short duration. During the Aerobic Exercises, warm up very slowly, building intensity very gradually. Then use a long aerobic cool-down while gradually reducing your exertion, slowly decreasing intensity.

Table 7.3
Cardiac Recovery Workout

Warm up very gradually, maintain a moderate pace, and cool down very slowly.

Thermal Warm-Up (10-15 minutes)	Move slowly and build very gradually.	
	Move #2	Pedal Jog: 30 seconds
	Move #3	Pomp & Circumstance: 8 times in each direction
	Move #1	Water Walk: very slowly for 60 seconds
	Move #4	Knee Lift Jog/March: 30 seconds as a nonbouncing march
	Move #9	Heel Jacks: 8 times
	Move #10	Alternate Leg Press Backs: 8 times
	Move #29	Snake Walk: Very slowly for 2 minutes

(continued)

Table 7.3 (*continued*)

Warm-Up Stretch (5-10 minutes)	Hold each stretch position for 10 seconds and breathe deeply.

Move #12   Outer Thigh Stretch
Move #13   Lower Back Stretch With Ankle Rotation
Move #14   Front of the Thigh Stretch
Move #15   Shin Stretch and Shoulder Shrug
Move #16   Inner Thigh Step Out
Move #17   Hip Flexor Stretch
Move #18   Straight Leg Calf Stretch
Move #19   Bent Knee Calf Stretch
Move #20   Hamstring Stretch

(Repeat previous sequence for other side of body.)

Move #21   Deep Muscle Buttocks Stretch
Move #22   Full Back Stretch
Move #23   Mid-Back Stretch
Move #24   Elbow Press Back
Move #25   Chest Stretch With Shoulder Rolls
Move #26   Upper Back Stretch
Move #27   Torso and Shoulder Stretch
Move #28   Shoulder and Upper Arm Stretch

Muscle Strengthening and Toning Exercises (10 minutes)

Begin with fewer repetitions and add more as the weeks progress. Breathe deeply during every exercise.

Move #50   Standing Crunch: 8-16 times
Move #51   Floating Curl: 8-16 times
Move #53   Outer/Inner Thigh Scissors: 8-16 times
Move #54   Forward and Back Leg Glide: 8-16 times per side
Move #55   Knee Kicks: 8-16 times per side
Move #58   Pivoted Dips: 4-8 times per side
Move #60   Calf Lifts: 8-16 times
Move #61   Toe Lifts: 8-16 times per foot
Move #62   Chest/Upper Back Glide: 8-16 times
Move #63   Chest/Back Press: 8-16 times

Move #65   Pivoted Shoulder Press: 8-16 times
Move #66   Side Arm Pump: 4-8 times
Move #67   Upper Arm Curls: 8-16 times
Move #69   Shoulder Shrugs and Rolls:
4-8 times each
Move #70   Behind-the-Back Press: 8 times

Aerobic Exercises

Start with 5 minutes and gradually build to 30 minutes over a period of 15 weeks. Your physician may recommend gradually lengthening the aerobic duration to an hour or more. In this section begin slowly, build progressively to a moderate aerobic exertion, then gradually decrease intensity.

Move #2   Pedal Jog: 30 seconds
Move #3   Pomp & Circumstance: 8 times in each direction
Move #1   Water Walk: 60 seconds
Move #4   Knee Lift Jog/March: March for 30 seconds
Move #9   Heel Jacks: 8 times
Move #10   Alternate Leg Press Backs: 8 times
Move #29   Snake Walk: 1-2 minutes
Move #30   Step Wide Side: 8 times in each direction
Move #31   Hydro Jacks: 8-16 times
Move #32   Cross-Country Ski: 16 times
Move #33   Sailor's Jig: 8-16 times
Move #41   Jump Twist: 8 times
Move #42   Aqua Ski: 10-30 seconds
Move #43   Floating Side Scissors: 10-30 seconds
Move #44   Back Float Kick and Squiggle: 10-30 seconds
Move #46   Vertical Flutter Kicks: 10-30 seconds
Move #47   Floating Mountain Climb: 30-60 seconds
Move #48   Bicycle Pump: 10-30 seconds
Move #49   Can-Can Soccer Kick: 10-30 seconds

(continued)

Table 7.3   (*continued*)

	Move #29	Snake Walk: 1-2 minutes
	Move #30	Step Wide Side: 8 times right, 8 times left. Repeat.
	Move #10	Alternate Leg Press Backs: 8 times
	Move #9	Heel Jacks: 8 times
	Move #4	Knee Lift Jog/March: March for 15-30 seconds
	Move #1	Water Walk: 1-2 minutes
	Move #3	Pomp & Circumstance: 8 times in each direction
	Move #2	Pedal Jog: 30 seconds
Final Cool-Down Stretches (10 minutes)	Repeat Warm-Up Stretch sequence, but hold each stretch for 20 to 30 seconds. Add these two Final Cool-Down Stretches:	
	Move #72	Safe Neck Stretch
	Move #73	Shoulder Hug

Water Exercise and Prenatal Fitness

Keeping in shape during pregnancy can have several benefits. During pregnancy a woman can anticipate a gradual potential weight gain (ideally) of 20 to 25 pounds, with its inevitable stress on the back. Pregnant women need muscle strengthening exercise to help them carry their increased body weight better, and afterward to help them carry the baby. Some physicians used to discourage weight training for fear of injuries due to softening of the ligaments and changes in the body's center of gravity associated with pregnancy. However, studies of muscle strengthening during pregnancy now show that such injuries are rare, probably because women who experience joint pain or balance problems stop whatever is causing them discomfort.

Labor itself presents a physical challenge of substantial proportions for most women. With a first pregnancy, women can expect to spend an average of 17 hours in labor. Women who have been exercising during pregnancy enjoy greater stamina during labor, are less likely to require medical intervention, and enjoy a quicker return to prepregnancy fitness levels following the birth. After the birth, mothers who exercised during pregnancy may be able to handle the stresses of motherhood better than women who avoided physical activity.

Studies by Dr. Robert G. McMurray examined the effects of land-based and water exercise on pregnant women. Exercising in the water reduced thermal stress (kept the future mother's temperature within safer levels for the fetus) and reduced her blood pressure and heart rate. The buoyancy of the water unloads the weight of the pregnancy, making exercise a much more comfortable choice for pregnant women.

Water also eliminates the danger of jumping or jarring. The cushioning, cooling effects of water make aquatic aerobic activity ideal for pregnant women. While water minimizes the potentially hazardous effects of over-exertion during pregnancy, it is still very important to warm up and cool down gradually and limit vigorous aerobic activity to 15 minutes at a time. Breathing fully and evenly will encourage proper oxygen delivery to your system.

Pregnant women who wish to engage in prenatal exercise activities should have the approval of their medical caregivers. Unless a woman has a history of miscarriage or spontaneous abortions, is experiencing vaginal bleeding, or has some other serious medical condition, exercise should become a routine from the beginning of pregnancy or, better yet, prior to pregnancy. According to Barbara B. Holstein, MS, of the International Childbirth Education Association, exercise delivers real bonuses for pregnant women: It reduces many of the common discomforts of pregnancy, helps prepare the mother-to-be for the rigors of birth, and eases the postpartum experience. Holstein has identified several specific benefits. They include:

1. Exercise improves circulation and builds muscular strength, which in turn reduces the pain, discomfort and severity of varicose veins, commonly suffered by pregnant women.
2. Exercise can help correct posture problems associated with pregnancy and prevent back pain by reducing muscular imbalance and enhancing strength.
3. Exercise can alleviate the discomfort and immobility of swollen joints by increasing circulation, thereby abating the edema (swelling caused by collection of fluids in the tissues) brought on by pregnancy.
4. Exercise can help to ease digestive discomforts and constipation.
5. Exercise with a flexed ankle instead of pointed toes can help reduce leg cramps. Flex at your ankle by lifting your toes toward your shin.
6. Exercise will strengthen the abdominal and thigh muscles, essential during the second stage of labor (when the baby passes through the birth canal).
7. Firm abdominals return to normal more readily after childbirth. Additionally, exercise helps women cope with postpartum baby blues.
8. Exercise helps a pregnant woman feel good about herself and move with grace and greater agility.

Certain activities can be beneficial during pregnancy, while others should be avoided. The American College of Obstetricians and Gynecologists (ACOG) has developed a number of guidelines for pregnant women to follow when exercising.

1. The mother-to-be should monitor her heart rate regularly during a workout and not allow it to exceed 140 beats per minute.
2. She should not exercise strenuously or in the aerobic heart rate zone for more than 15 minutes at a time.
3. She needs to drink plenty of water before, during, and after a workout.
4. She should avoid all jumping and jarring movements and rapid changes in direction.
5. She should avoid exercise during very hot or humid weather.
6. After the fourth month, she should not exercise flat on her back.
7. Stretches should not be taken to the maximum point of resistance.

The ACOG recommends shorter, lower intensity aerobic segments because prolonged high intensity exercise diverts oxygen carrying blood away from the uterus to the muscles and the skin, and can result in smaller than normal babies. Energy production raises the body temperature during exercise, a condition called hyperthermia, and may cause a wide variety of spinal cord abnormalities and faulty brain and skull development of the fetus. To help regulate temperature, pregnant women who exercise should consume more fluids, especially water. Remember, the water itself provides a cooling environment.

The reason for avoiding exercise on the back after the fourth month, says ACOG, is to prevent the enlarged uterus from obstructing the vena cava, a major vein that returns blood to the heart. It is believed that laying flat on your back after the first trimester can cause compression of the vena cava, which reduces the flow of oxygen-rich blood to the uterus. Let your doctor and your comfort level be your guides. Also, because hormones emitted during pregnancy encourage softening of the ligaments, it is important to stretch gently to avoid damaging the ligaments and joints.

Most experts recommend exercise prior to pregnancy because if you start out in good shape, you'll have an easier time staying in shape. Sports gynecologist Mona Shangold suggests that, for women with normal, uncomplicated pregnancies, it is "probably reasonable to continue exercising at the same level of exertion you were accustomed to before pregnancy, but it may not be safe to exercise more vigorously or more frequently than that."

The same level of exertion may not mean the same level of intensity or frequency. You may have to make adjustments to your exercise program as the pregnancy progresses to compensate for weight gain. The additional weight increases your work load, so you may need to reduce the intensity and the frequency of exercise to continue exercising at the same level of exertion you did before you gained the weight.

Ratings of perceived exertion, that is, judging by how you feel, may be a safer means of measuring your intensity level than monitoring your heart rate. IDEA, the international association of fitness professionals, recommends use of the perceived exertion scale because it encourages you to take note of how hard your changing system is working. Or use the talk test to keep your activity within aerobic intensity limits. If you cannot carry on a slightly breathy conversation during exercise, you are exercising too hard.

Keep in mind that your pregnant body still sends you signals, though it may not say the same things it did during your prepregnancy workouts. High-spirited physical enthusiasm usually gives way to the wisdom that it is best not to push it. The key is, if you have learned to listen to your nonpregnant body, your pregnant one will provide you with important information as well.

Pregnancy Workout

Moderation is the key for any prenatal exercise program. Maternal pulse and blood pressure rise more quickly during exercise, and you may not be able to deliver oxygen to your working muscles as quickly as usual. You may find that you fatigue more quickly as a result. Sudden bursts of high-energy exercise or prolonged workouts are inappropriate. Follow the adage, "If it hurts, don't do it."

Eat a small, nutritious snack (low fat, high complex carbohydrate) about an hour before you exercise and a well-balanced meal after you are through. Limiting food intake so that you burn the body's own stores is absolutely not appropriate because it can be detrimental to the fetus.

Holstein recommends the following guidelines:

- Avoid rapid twisting movements, jumps, or rapid shifts in direction, level, or speed.
- Exclude any exercises that cause hyperextension of any joint or flexion taken beyond the maximum point of resistance.
- Do not let your back sag or arch.
- Eliminate exercises that require you to bend forward at the hip with a straight back. If both feet are on the floor, forward flexion should always be performed with bent knees.

Use the Pregnancy Workout version of the Basic Water Workout routine in Table 7.4 and concentrate on making adjustments based on the previous recommendations. Stop any exercise that feels uncomfortable or painful.

Table 7.4
Pregnancy Workout

Thermal Warm-Up (5 minutes)	Start slowly and build very gradually.

	Move #2	Pedal Jog: 30 seconds
	Move #3	Pomp & Circumstance: 8 times in each direction
	Move #1	Water Walk: Very slowly for 60 seconds
	Move #4	Knee Lift Jog/March: 15 seconds as a nonbouncing march
	Move #10	Alternate Leg Press Backs: 16 times
	Move #29	Snake Walk: Very slowly for 2 minutes

Warm-Up Stretch (5 minutes)	Hold each stretch position for 10 seconds.

	Move #12	Outer Thigh Stretch
	Move #13	Lower Back Stretch With Ankle Rotation
	Move #14	Front of the Thigh Stretch
	Move #15	Shin Stretch and Shoulder Shrug
	Move #16	Inner Thigh Step Out
	Move #17	Hip Flexor Stretch
	Move #18	Straight Leg Calf Stretch
	Move #19	Bent Knee Calf Stretch
	Move #20	Hamstring Stretch

(Repeat previous sequence for other side of body.)

	Move #21	Deep Muscle Buttocks Stretch
	Move #22	Full Back Stretch
	Move #23	Mid-Back Stretch (eliminate the first position)
	Move #24	Elbow Press Back
	Move #25	Chest Stretch With Shoulder Rolls
	Move #26	Upper Back Stretch
	Move #27	Torso and Shoulder Stretch
	Move #28	Shoulder and Upper Arm Stretch

Aerobic Exercises	Warm up gradually, maintain a moderate pace, and cool down slowly. Limit your aerobic exertion to 15 minutes at a time.

Move #2   Pedal Jog: 30 seconds

Move #3   Pomp & Circumstance: 8 times in each direction

Move #1   Water Walk: 60 seconds

Move #4   Knee Lift Jog/March: 15 seconds as a nonbouncing march

Move #10   Alternate Leg Press Backs: 16 times

Move #30   Step Wide Side: 8 times in each direction

Move #29   Snake Walk: 1-2 minutes

Flotation Exercises: Use two empty plastic water jugs or upper arm flotation cuffs such as the Hydro-Fit Flotation Cuffs or the Sprint Adult Water Wings.

Move #42   Aqua Ski: 10-30 seconds

Move #43   Floating Side Scissors: 10-30 seconds

Move #45   Vertical Frog Bob: 8 times

Move #46   Vertical Flutter Kicks: 10-30 seconds

Move #47   Floating Mountain Climb: 30-60 seconds

Move #48   Bicycle Pump: 10-30 seconds

Move #49   Can-Can Soccer Kick: 10-30 seconds

Move #29   Snake Walk: 1-2 minutes

Move #30   Step Wide Side: 8 times right, 8 times left. Repeat.

Move #10   Alternate Leg Press Backs: 16 times

Move #4   Knee Lift Jog/March: 15-30 seconds as a nonbouncing march

Move #1   Water Walk: 1-2 minutes

Move #3   Pomp & Circumstance: 8 times in each direction

Move #2   Pedal Jog: 30 seconds

Muscle Strengthening and Toning Exercises (5-10 minutes)	Begin with fewer repetitions and add more as the weeks progress.
	Move #50 Standing Crunch: 8-16 times

(continued)

Table 7.4   *(continued)*

	Move #52 Sitting "V": 6-16 times
	Move #53 Outer/Inner Thigh Scissors: 8-16 times
	Move #54 Forward and Back Leg Glide: 8-16 times per side
	Move #55 Knee Kicks: 8-16 times per side
	Move #57 Hip Side Press: 8 times
	Move #59 Supported Squats: 8-16 times
	Move #60 Calf Lifts: 8-16 times
	Move #61 Toe Lifts: 8-16 times per foot
	Move #62 Chest/Upper Back Glide: 8-16 times
	Move #63 Chest/Back Press: 8-16 times
	Move #65 Pivoted Shoulder Press: 8-16 times
	Move #66 Side Arm Pump: 4-8 times
	Move #67 Upper Arm Curls: 8-16 times
	Move #69 Shoulder Shrugs and Rolls: 4-8 times each
	Move #71 Cat Back Press: 8-16 times
Final Cool-Down Stretches (10-15 minutes)	Repeat Warm-Up Stretch sequence, but hold each stretch for 20-30 seconds. Add this Final Cool-Down Stretch:
	Move #72 Safe Neck Stretch

Your exercise sequences should emphasize movements that strengthen the back and abdominals. The lunge and moves such as the Alternate Leg Press Backs are particularly helpful because they strengthen the muscles while promoting balance and alignment. Eliminate fast turning motions in side and forward lunges.

Use the Final Cool-Down section to teach your mind and body to relax as well as to maintain flexibility. Tension reduction skills and the ability to consciously relax will come in handy during childbirth when you will need to relax during labor contractions. You can develop basic relaxation skills by focusing your attention on softening the muscle involved in each stretch. Consciously allow the muscle fibers to unwind, and breathe deeply. Imagine that you can bring your breath right to the muscle you are relaxing, and exhale deeply. This method of "conscious release" can be used for every part of your body and will help you eliminate tightness and tension. Use pleasant, soothing instrumental music. You may wish to perform these relaxation exercises outside the pool in a lounge chair under warm towels if your body feels too cool.

Exercise for Older Adults

Adults in the prime of life need more time to warm up, and must cool down more gradually. As we get older, sudden strenuous exercise can be hazardous to the heart. A 10- to 15-minute Thermal Warm-Up at the beginning of your aerobic sequence will help prepare your joints and muscles for greater exertion and gradually increase the circulation and heart rate. A moderate aerobic intensity level produces the most beneficial gains in overall fitness, according to exercise physiologists Kenneth Cooper and Steven Blair. During the Water Aerobics section, warm up slowly, then continue to build very gradually and monitor your intensity, working toward a moderate level of perceived exertion. Decrease intensity when warranted by taking smaller steps, reducing resistance (for example, sliding through the water with a slicing hand position instead of cupped hands—see p. 72), moving more slowly, and minimizing bouncing. Use these same techniques to cool down at the end of your Water Aerobics segment. Abrupt cessation of vigorous exercise can cause pooling of the blood in the limbs, which places unnecessary strain on the heart while the body works to divert the blood back to your trunk. To prevent this unwanted stress on your cardiovascular system, your cool-down period at the end of Water Aerobics should gradually reduce intensity over a period of at least 10 minutes. By cooling down gradually you can prevent muscle soreness after exercise.

Regulating body temperature can be more challenging for older adults. If you tend to cool easily, wear long sleeves and tights, such as the chlorine-resistant bodysuits manufactured by WaterWear in New Hampshire, U.S.A. (see page 19). Drink plenty of cool (but not cold) water before, during, and after your workout to help regulate your body temperature effectively and to prevent early onset of fatigue. Icy water can be more difficult to absorb and can cause cramping.

A fully rounded workout will help you improve or maintain flexibility, keep you strong and physically independent, improve the health and longevity of your heart, lungs, and circulatory system, and give you renewed energy and vigor. Proper body posture, warm-up, cool-down, and flexibility exercises as described in the Basic Water Workout will help prevent muscle soreness.

If you are just getting back into shape, you may choose to start your new water workout program with a sequence that does not include aerobic conditioning until you strengthen your muscles a bit. (See "Initial Conditioning Stage," page 20.) A beginning sequence of this type may include Thermal Warm-Up, Warm-Up Stretch, Strengthening and Toning, and Final Cool-Down Stretches. After you gain a sense of balance and strength in the water, add a Water Aerobics section of about 5 to 10 minutes' duration. Follow the "Water Workout for Older Adults" format described in Table 7.5, and plug in your favorite exercises from the Basic Water Workout exercise descriptions. Use the nonbouncing, low impact variation of each exercise. If one exercise doesn't feel right, try another one until you find those you like. Be sure to perform all the stretching exercises and to stretch only to the comfortable point of resistance.

Table 7.5
Water Workout for Older Adults

Component	Duration

Thermal Warm-Up   *10 minutes*

Water walking is an excellent warm-up for older adults. Concentrate on using proper body position. Walk slowly forward and backward and pedal jog lightly during this warm-up. Omit backward walking if you have balance problems. You may use aqua shoes or an old pair of lightweight canvas sneakers to improve traction, stability, and movement confidence.

Warm-Up Stretch   *5 minutes*

Complete the entire stretch sequence. Study and emulate the position instructions carefully and avoid stretching beyond a comfortable and normal range of motion. You may wish to eliminate the "keep warm" upper and lower body motions in order to focus on your stretch stability. Therefore, try to locate a pool environment that you find comfortably warm.

Water Aerobics   *Build up to 20-30 minutes**

Start out very slowly and use the first 10 minutes to gradually elevate your intensity to a moderate, comfortable level. Monitor your intensity carefully. Avoid impact in your movements by eliminating hops, bounces, and jumps. During the last 10 minutes, gradually lower your intensity until your breathing is smooth, even, and unlabored. Eliminate any aerobic exercises that feel too strenuous or uncomfortable. Build to longer duration over a period of months if weight control is an objective.

Strengthening and Toning Exer-   10-15 minutes
cises

Perform each of the exercises in a slow, controlled manner. Start with 8 repetitions of each exercise and build to 16 or more over a period of months or years. Pay close attention to your body position and stability. Eliminate

Component	Duration

any exercises that feel uncomfortable and try them again at a later date when you are stronger.

Final Cool-Down Stretches   *10-15 minutes*

Complete all of the final Cool-Down Stretches, checking your position to ensure proper body alignment. Hold each stretch for 10 to 30 seconds. If a stretch position is uncomfortable, check your position again and ease up on the stretch by reducing the extent or degree of the stretch. For instance, if your calf feels tight during a calf stretch, bring your front and back foot a bit closer together to reduce the stretch. If it still causes discomfort, eliminate that particular stretch and try it at a later date when your flexibility improves overall.

*Remember, you have the option of starting out with 5-10 minutes of aerobic exercise and gradually adding a minute each week.

You will need a day of rest between bouts of exercise to build your strength and prevent pain or injury from overuse. Exercise every other day, starting with 5 or 10 minutes if you have been inactive for a number of years, and add a minute each week until you reach a duration you find comfortable. A good objective for cardiovascular health and overall fitness would be to build toward 20 to 30 minutes of aerobic exercise per session. However, adding even a few minutes at a time can effectively improve your cardiovascular health. Remember, begin each session with Thermal Warm-Up and Warm-Up Stretches and finish every workout with the complete array of Final Cool-Down Stretches.

Arthritis Aquatics

More than 360 million people worldwide, or 10% of the world's population, have arthritis, according to Glenn McWaters, author of *Deep Water Exercise for Health & Fitness*. Because hydrodynamics reduces joint stress and weight bearing, exercise performed in the water is considered one of the most universally beneficial methods for managing all types of arthritis.

There are more than 100 different kinds of arthritis. Most are characterized by inflammation of the joints, which causes painful swelling and can result in loss of joint motion or function. With proper diagnosis and treatment, joint damage caused by arthritis can be limited or prevented, and joint motion and flexibility can be improved. Because there are many ways to minimize pain and loss of motion from arthritis, people with arthritis need to work with their health professionals to determine the treatment program that is best for them. Most experience relief with regular water activity. In fact, water activity is considered the best therapy for osteoarthritis or Rheumutoid arthritis, according to Edward A. Abraham, orthopaedic surgeon and author of *Freedom from Back Pain*.

Pain in your joints may make you want to hold them very still. But not using your joints will cause the joints, ligaments, and muscles to lose range of motion and weaken over time. Immobility may also cause muscles to shorten and tighten up, causing you to feel more pain and stiffness and limiting your ability to do the things you want to do.

Regular exercise helps keep the joints moving. It restores and preserves flexibility and strength, and can protect against further damage. Because exercise helps improve coordination, endurance, and mobility, it makes you feel good about yourself and your ability to accomplish more. Water provides a comfortable way for people with arthritis to exercise gently and without pain. The buoyancy of the water supports the body, lessens stress on the joints, and frees movement for greater range of motion. Water also acts as a force of resistance to help build muscle strength.

If you have arthritis, you should exercise daily for approximately 45 minutes to maintain and improve flexibility, strength, and endurance. Fifteen minutes three times a day may work better in many cases than 45 minutes all at once. To achieve maximum benefit, fully submerge the joint you are working. Submerging the joint will relieve it from the stress of gravity, and the buoyancy should help you move that part of your body through its full, normal range of motion. Exercise intensity should be determined by the level of pain tolerance you may be experiencing on a given day. Actively inflamed joints may become worse with excessive exercise; therefore, exercise should be greatly reduced during inflammatory episodes.

Here are some special precautions people with arthritis should take, recommended by the Arthritis Foundation:

1. Consult your doctor to determine whether water exercises are appropriate for you.
2. Be sure that someone else is nearby to help you in and out of the pool, if necessary.
3. Check the temperature before you enter the pool. The water temperature should feel soothing and comfortable, not hot. Temperatures between 83 and 88 degrees Fahrenheit or 28 to 31 degrees centigrade are appropriate for exercisers with arthritis.
4. If you feel light-headed or nauseated, you should carefully get out of the water immediately.
5. If joint swelling, stiffness, or pain increases, discontinue exercise and consult your doctor.
6. Never enter a pool after using alcohol or drugs. The sleepiness, drowsiness, and raised or lowered blood pressure that can result

could cause injury or even death. If you are taking medication, consult your doctor before entering the pool to exercise.

7. Start slowly and don't overdo it. Learn to recognize your body's reactions to exercise and stop activities *before* you become fatigued. Arthritis symptoms flare up and disappear over time, so exercises that feel easy one day may feel difficult the next. Change your exercise program so that it takes your current symptoms into account.

8. Pay close attention to pain signals. If you continue to exercise when you feel pain, you may cause further damage.

If warm water makes your arthritis feel better, this is the best workout for you. Make sure your pool temperature is 83 to 88 degrees Fahrenheit or 28 to 31 degrees centigrade before you enter the water. Relax and enjoy the soothing sensation of the water. When your muscles and joints feel comfortable and free of tension, begin your exercise routine slowly. Give yourself enough time after exercising to completely relax your muscles before you get out of the water. You can exercise in warmer water if no aerobic exercise is planned.

The Arthritis Foundation provides important guidelines for water exercises:

- Submerge the body part that you plan to exercise.
- Move that body part slowly and gently.
- Breathe in a normal, deep rhythmic pattern and avoid holding your breath.
- Start and finish with simple exercises.
- Alternate between difficult activities and simple ones to minimize fatigue.
- Use flotation devices to help conserve your energy.
- Do not add resistance equipment unless your doctor has instructed you to do so. If you use resistance equipment at all, employ low resistance versions.
- Avoid gripping the pool edge or equipment tightly. Hold on to the pool wall gently or place your elbow on the edge to improve stability during wall exercises.
- Move through the complete range of motion around your joint. Do not force movement. Stop if you feel sudden or increased pain.
- Complete three to eight repetitions, based on what works best for you. Over time, gradually increase the number of repetitions to 15 if you find that the increase is well tolerated.
- If a particular exercise is uncomfortable for you, don't do it. If it hurts, stop.
- Pain that lasts for more than one to two hours after exercise may

signal overuse. Cut back the next time you exercise. If pain persists after cutting back, change the exercise.

- Begin gradually and slowly. Don't overdo. Do not perform more repetitions than you are comfortable with.
- If you have severe joint damage or joint replacement, you should check with your doctor or surgeon before you do any of the exercises.

The exercise program in Table 7.6 can be performed while standing or sitting in the pool or while using flotation equipment. For detailed instructions on the exercises, consult Part II, "Performing Water Exercises." Include the moves numbered 74 to 77 if arthritis affects your hands and feet.

Table 7.6
Arthritis Workout

Thermal Warm-Up: (5 minutes)	Choose one or more of the following.

	Move #1	Water Walk
	Move #4	Knee Lift Jog/March
	Move #5	Toy Soldier March
	Move #30	Step Wide Side

Warm-Up Stretch: (5 minutes)	Complete all the stretches that you find comfortable. Hold each stretch lightly for 10 seconds. Stretching should *never* be painful.

	Move #12	Outer Thigh Stretch
	Move #13	Lower Back Stretch With Ankle Rotation
	Move #14	Front of the Thigh Stretch
	Move #15	Shin Stretch and Shoulder Shrug
	Move #16	Inner Thigh Step Out
	Move #17	Hip Flexor Stretch
	Move #18	Straight Leg Calf Stretch
	Move #19	Bent Knee Calf Stretch
	Move #20	Hamstring Stretch

(Repeat previous sequence for other side of body.)

	Move #21	Deep Muscle Buttocks Stretch
	Move #23	Mid-Back Stretch (3 parts)
	Move #24	Elbow Press Back
	Move #25	Chest Stretch With Shoulder Rolls

Move #26   Upper Back Stretch
Move #27   Torso and Shoulder Stretch
Move #28   Shoulder and Upper Arm Stretch

Aerobic Exercises With
Flotation
(5-15 minutes)

This segment is optional and should be performed only when you are not tired. Remember, warm up and cool down gradually and perform the exercises at the speed that feels most comfortable to you. Use a flotation belt, vest, upper arm cuffs, or adult water wings.

Move #42   Aqua Ski
Move #43   Floating Side Scissors
Move #45   Vertical Frog Bob
Move #48   Bicycle Pump

Range of Motion and
Strengthening Exercises:
(15-20 minutes)

Move #53   Outer/Inner Thigh Scissors
Move #54   Forward and Back Leg Glide
Move #55   Knee Kicks
Move #56   Runner's Stride
Move #57   Hip Side Press
Move #58   Pivoted Dips
Move #59   Supported Squats
Move #62   Chest/Upper Back Glide
Move #63   Chest/Back Press
Move #64   Diagonal Front Shoulder Press
Move #65   Pivoted Shoulder Press
Move #66   Side Arm Pump
Move #67   Upper Arm Curls
Move #68   Traffic Cop
Move #69   Shoulder Shrugs and Rolls
Move #70   Behind-the-Back Press
Move #74   Finger Curl (p. 146)
Move #75   Finger Touch (p. 146)
Move #76   Thumb Circles (p. 147)
Move #60   Calf Lifts
Move #61   Toe Lifts
Move #77   Toe Curls (p. 147)

Final Cool-Down
Stretches
(10 minutes)

Perform the same stretches recommended during Warm-Up, but hold the static stretch positions for 20 seconds. Add these two Final Cool-Down Stretches.

Move #72   Safe Neck Stretch
Move #73   Shoulder Hug

Move #74: Finger Curl

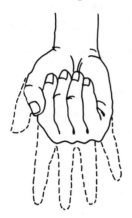

Action: Open and close your palms slowly. Make a loose fist.

Variation: Bend the larger knuckles of all four fingers and bring your fingertips toward the tops of your palms.

Move #75: Finger Touch

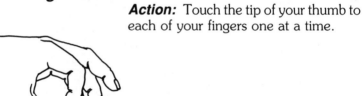

Action: Touch the tip of your thumb to each of your fingers one at a time.

Move #76: Thumb Circles

Action: Make large circles with your thumb.

Move #77: Toe Curls

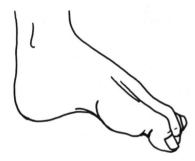

Action: Curl your toes down and then straighten them out. Exercise one foot at a time.

Enhancing Physical Rehabilitation

Water has been used for its healing properties since ancient times. Roman armies treated wounded soldiers in hot springs. Today aqua therapy is used to treat people with a wide variety of injuries and disabilities.

Water exercise for rehabilitation can be enjoyed by most people, but it is especially well suited to people with joint pain, orthopedic difficulties, weight problems, movement limitations, or lower back pain. People who derive the greatest benefits include post-surgical patients, chronic pain patients, and elite athletes.

Aqua therapy programs make use of water's basic physical properties of specific gravity, buoyancy, hydrostatic pressure (which keeps an equal amount of pressure on all joints in water), and viscosity (resistance). Rehabilitative aqua exercise uses these properties creatively to increase balanced strength and flexibility; to improve coordination, movement skills, and cardiopulmonary functioning (strengthen the heart, lungs, and circulatory system); and to promote relaxation and a sense of well-being.

Therapists working with recovering individuals use the aquatic environment because water's buoyancy minimizes pressure on all the joints and muscles. For example, when you are chest-deep in water, your body becomes 90% buoyant, so you only have to move and support 10% of your body weight. Consequently, water makes it possible for people recovering from almost any injury to handle exercise and fitness programs they cannot perform on land, speeding up the often long rehabilitation and healing process. In addition, the movement of exercise and the warm water increase circulation to the injured area, boosting the body's healing mechanisms.

Water offers a safe, protective environment for therapeutic exercise for several other reasons. In water, there is very little negative stress or wear and tear on the body. With proper warm-up and cool-down, water reduces the likelihood of injuries or reinjuries because it eases the actions of the joints even though it makes the body work harder. When you walk on land, there is less resistance to your movement, and you are able to swing your arms and move your legs freely. In water, you must fight against the resistance of the water to maintain your balance. By working against the resistance (positive stress), you build strength, coordination, and endurance.

For those who need to lose weight to restore mobility and good health, aquatic rehabilitation makes sense because working out in water burns up more calories in less time than performing similar exercise on dry land. A 30-minute workout in water, according to the Physical Therapy Forum (1989), can be equivalent to a 45-minute session on land, making it an excellent way to obtain a regular cardiovascular, fat-burning workout.

Physical therapists tell numerous success stories. For example, Mary weighed close to 300 pounds when she started a weight reduction program. She was on the right track when she tried to incorporate aerobic exercise with a diet plan, but was held back by pain in the knees, shins, ankles, and back: pain brought on by her excessive weight. On the recommendation of her physical therapist, Mary tried water aerobics and loved it. She lost 100 pounds (45 kg) in eleven months and had no injuries. Another rehabilitation client, Bob, broke his left knee and hip in a sport accident. His recovery was slow until he began aquatic exercise therapy. The buoyant, warm-water environment enabled him to exercise for longer periods and accelerated his healing.

Igor Burdenko, one of the most dynamic leaders in the field of water therapy, has a talent for getting injured athletes back on their feet. His unique exercise methods have earned him a glowing reputation among professional atheltes such as Kevin McHale, a celebrated NBA basketball player. McHale employed Burdenko's water methods and recovered from foot surgery months earlier than doctors had predicted.

Burdenko's healing talents stem from more than 20 years of research and experimentation in the field of rehabilitative science, most of which focused on water therapy. His pool-based techniques make use of flotation vests, which keep the wearer vertical and weightless. Burdenko's exercises create a natural traction on bones, joints, and connective tissue. The neutral buoyancy allows you to relax and bob up and down comfortably. The relaxed position is not possible in a traditional life vest, which forces the body to tense. Warmer water temperatures (84 to 94 degrees Fahrenheit or 29 to 34 degrees centigrade) and relaxed postures during exercise, says Burdenko, improve circulation to injured areas and promote the healing process. His exercise sessions involve walking or running backward and forward in an upright position with flotation, without touching the bottom. Burdenko points out that water workouts involve natural movements that can imitate your sport. A tennis player, for instance, can practice his forehand or backhand racquet motion; a golfer, her driving swing; or a softball player, the motion of batting or pitching.

Burdenko also achieves astounding results using kick boards and flotation barbells to aid in balance and create resistance during exercises. For instance, Harvey Schwartz, a 41-year-old lawyer, injured his back one morning while reaching across the kitchen table for a newspaper and could barely move when he sought treatment with Burdenko. After just two weeks of recuperative water exercise, Harvey was, in his own words, "out in the woods cutting down trees."

Burdenko adheres to a number of important guidelines: Primarily, the former Russian national avoids pain. "In America, there used to be a saying: No pain, no gain. In 22 years, I have never known an example where pain heals," he observes. He never has a client work immediately on the injured area. Instead, Burdenko recommends, first work the muscles around an injury. Later, when you have gained enough strength, he recommends, exercise the injured area.

Another of Burdenko's imperatives is to work symmetrically. He explains, "You must work the muscles in all directions to develop harmony. And work simply—simple motion, simple equipment, simple exercise." Continuing to exercise throughout the healing process also is critical. Though doctors frequently prescribe complete rest following injury, appropriate recuperative exercise produces healing circulation that cannot be generated if you do not combine recovery exercise with adequate rest.

Therapeutic water exercise is recommended for people with multiple sclerosis (MS) because it gives them a greater sense of control over their bodies. If you have multiple sclerosis, you could benefit from performing the Back and Neck Pain Workout. Water workouts can help individuals with MS to maintain or improve physical mobility, increase flexibility, gain muscle strength, improve balance and coordination, and manage stress. However, pushing too hard can bring on symptoms and hasten the progression of the disorder.

Specific workouts for enhancing injury recovery appear in Tables 7.7 through 7.9. Review the exercise recommendations with your doctor or physical therapist to make sure that they are right for you. Then follow the exercise sequence appropriate for your needs two to three times per week, taking at least one day of rest between workouts to ensure healing. Gradually build your duration and intensity as your condition improves.

Move #78: Shoulder Circles

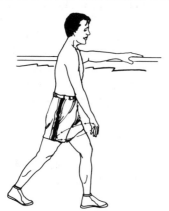

Starting Position: Stand with your left side next to the pool wall. Place your left foot forward and your right foot back. Secure the braced neutral position. Place your left elbow and forearm on the pool edge and let your right arm hang down toward the floor.

Action:

1. Circle your arm slowly in small, counterclockwise circles, then in clockwise circles.
2. Turn around and repeat using the other arm. Repeat 4 to 32 times in each direction with each arm.

Table 7.7
The Back and Neck Pain Workout

Perform this sequence when you are feeling relatively well. Rest when you are experiencing severe pain. Your doctor may recommend that you use a frozen gel pack on your painful areas before and after exercise to minimize inflammation.

Thermal Warm-Up (5-10 minutes)	Repeat this Thermal Warm-Up sequence 2-3 times.

	Move #1	Water Walk: 1 minute
	Move #3	Pomp & Circumstance: 8 times forward, 8 times backward (if balance permits)
	Move #4	Knee Lift Jog/March: Nonbouncing march for 15 seconds
	Move #10	Alternate Leg Press Backs: 8-16 times, no bouncing. (Perform facing the pool wall or ladder and hold on with both hands. Omit ladder/wall hold if you have neck pain.)

Warm-Up Stretch (5-10 minutes)	Take your time getting into each position and hold each stretch for 10 seconds. It is essential to perform every stretch indicated. Stability is critical, so use the wall for support and follow the instructions for the braced neutral position on pages 21 through 22 very carefully. If the stretch is uncomfortable, reduce the amount of stretch and double check your position. Do not use the arm movements designed to keep your body warm. If you get cool, find a warmer pool or wear chlorine-resistant lycra tights or a bodysuit.

	Move #12	Outer Thigh Stretch
	Move #13	Lower Back Stretch With Ankle Rotation
	Move #14	Front of the Thigh Stretch
	Move #15	Shin Stretch and Shoulder Shrug
	Move #16	Inner Thigh Step Out
	Move #17	Hip Flexor Stretch
	Move #18	Straight Leg Calf Stretch

(continued)

Table 7.7   *(continued)*

	Move #19	Bent Knee Calf Stretch
	Move #20	Hamstring Stretch

(Repeat previous sequence for other side of body.)

	Move #21	Deep Muscle Buttocks Stretch
	Move #22	Full Back Stretch (check with your physical therapist)
	Move #23	Mid-Back Stretch (3 parts)
	Move #24	Elbow Press Back
	Move #25	Chest Stretch With Shoulder Rolls
	Move #26	Upper Back Stretch
	Move #27	Torso and Shoulder Stretch
	Move #28	Shoulder and Upper Arm Stretch
	Move #72	Safe Neck Stretch
	Move #73	Shoulder Hug

Aerobic Exercises (1-30 minutes)	Optional. Pick and choose exercises you find comfortable from this list and perform them in the order provided.	
	Move #1	Water Walk: 1 minute
	Move #3	Pomp & Circumstance: 8 times forward, 8 times backward (if balance permits)
	Move #4	Knee Lift Jog/March: March for 15 seconds, no bouncing
	Move #10	Alternate Leg Press Backs: 8-16 times, no bouncing. (Perform facing the pool wall or ladder and hold on with both hands if you don't have neck pain.)
	Move #29	Snake Walk
	Move #30	Step Wide Side
Flotation Aerobics:	Move #42	Aqua Ski
	Move #43	Floating Side Scissors
	Move #44	Back Float Kick and Squiggle
	Move #46	Vertical Flutter Kicks
	Move #47	Floating Mountain Climb
	Move #48	Bicycle Pump

	Move #49	Can-Can Soccer Kick
	Move #29	Snake Walk
	Move #30	Step Wide Side
Muscle Strengthening and Toning Exercises	Move #50	The Standing Crunch: Perform 8-16 times with no resistance. Add resistance when you have reached a generally pain-free status.
	Move #51	Floating Curl: 8-16 times
	Move #52	Sitting "V": 8-16 times
	Move #53	Outer/Inner Thigh Scissors: 8-32 times
	Move #54	Forward and Back Leg Glide: 8-32 times
	Move #55	Knee Kicks: 8-16 times
	Move #56	Runner's Stride: 8-16 times
	Move #57	Hip Side Press: 8-32 times
	Move #58	Pivoted Dips: 4-8 times
	Move #59	Supported Squats: 8-32 times
	Move #60	Calf Lifts: 8-16 times
	Move #61	Toe Lifts: 8-16 times
	Move #62	Chest/Upper Back Glide: 8-16 times
	Move #63	Chest/Back Press: 8-32 times
	Move #65	Pivoted Shoulder Press: 8-32 times
	Move #67	Upper Arm Curls: 8-16 times
	Move #68	Traffic Cop: 8-32 times
	Move #69	Shoulder Shrugs and Rolls: 8-16 times
	Move #70	Behind-the-Back Press: 8-16 times
	Move #71	Cat Back Press: 8-16 times
Final Cool-Down Stretches (10 minutes)		Perform the same stretches recommended during Warm-Up, but hold the static stretch positions for 20 to 30 seconds.

Table 7.8
The Shoulder Pain Workout

The sequence illustrated is designed to help alleviate shoulder pain. Start with no equipment. As the routine begins to feel easy, gradually add webbed gloves, then wrist weights. To obtain a well-rounded workout, you may wish to include additional exercises from "The Back and Neck Pain Workout" (Table 7.7).

Thermal Warm-Up (5-10 minutes)	Repeat this Thermal Warm-Up sequence 2 to 3 times.

	Move #1	Water Walk: 1 minute
	Move #3	Pomp & Circumstance: 8 times forward, 8 times backward (if balance permits)
	Move #4	Knee Lift Jog/March: March for 15 seconds
	Move #10	Alternate Leg Press Backs: 8-16 times

Warm-Up Stretch (5-10 minutes)	Hold each stretch for 10 seconds and perform them in the order indicated.

	Move #23	Mid-Back Stretch (3 parts)
	Move #24	Elbow Press Back
	Move #25	Chest Stretch With Shoulder Rolls
	Move #26	Upper Back Stretch
	Move #27	Torso and Shoulder Stretch
	Move #22	Full Back Stretch
	Move #28	Shoulder and Upper Arm Stretch
	Move #72	Safe Neck Stretch
	Move #73	Shoulder Hug

Range of Motion and Muscle Strengthening Exercises	Perform these exercises slowly. Start with a low number of repetitions and build gradually.

	Move #62	Chest/Upper Back Glide: 4-32 times
	Move #63	Chest/Back Press: 4-32 times
	Move #64	Diagonal Front Shoulder Press: 4-32 times
	Move #65	Pivoted Shoulder Press: 4-32 times
	Move #66	Side Arm Pump: 4-32 times, both variations
	Move #67	Upper Arm Curls: 4-32 times
	Move #68	Traffic Cop: 4-32 times
	Move #69	Shoulder Shrugs and Rolls: 4-32 times

	Move #70	Behind-the-Back Press: 4-16 times
	Move #71	Cat Back Press: 8-16 times
	Move #78	Shoulder Circles: 4-32 times
Final Cool-Down Stretches (10-15 minutes)		Perform the same stretches recommended during Warm-Up, but hold the static stretch positions for 20 to 30 seconds.

Table 7.9
The Knee Pain Workout

Because weight gain is a factor in some knee pain situations, an optional aerobic section is included. Be sure to include upper body stretches if you perform upper body movements. Perform this sequence when you are feeling relatively well. Rest when you are experiencing severe pain. Your doctor may recommend that you use a frozen gel pack on your painful areas before and after exercise to minimize inflammation.

Thermal Warm-Up (5-10 minutes)		Perform this Thermal Warm-Up sequence two to three times.
	Move #1	Water Walk: 1 minute
	Move #3	Pomp & Circumstance: 8 times forward, 8 times backward
	Move #5	Toy Soldier March: 16 times forward, 16 times backward
	Move #10	Alternate Leg Press Backs: 8-16 times
Warm-Up Stretch (5-10 minutes)		Take your time getting into each position and hold each stretch for 10 seconds. Perform stretches that can be managed pain free.
	Move #12	Outer Thigh Stretch
	Move #13	Lower Back Stretch With Ankle Rotation
	Move #14	Front of the Thigh Stretch: Do not bend the knee beyond 90 degrees (right angle).
	Move #15	Shin Stretch *Without* Shoulder Shrugs
	Move #16	Inner Thigh Step Out
	Move #17	Hip Flexor Stretch
	Move #18	Straight Leg Calf Stretch

(continued)

Table 7.9   (continued)

	Move #19	Bent Knee Calf Stretch
	Move #20	Hamstring Stretch
	(Repeat previous sequence for other side of body.)	
	Move #21	Deep Muscle Buttocks Stretch
	Move #22	Full Back Stretch
	Move #23	Mid-Back Stretch (3 parts)
Aerobic Exercises (Optional: 5-30 minutes)	Move #1	Water Walk: 1 minute
	Move #3	Pomp & Circumstance: 8 times forward, 8 times backward
	Move #5	Toy Soldier March: 16-32 times forward and backward
	Move #10	Alternate Leg Press Backs: 16 times
	Move #30	Step Wide Side: 16-32 times (Keep your knees behind your toes by contracting the front and back of your thighs to stabilize your knee position.)
Flotation Aerobics:	Move #42	Aqua Ski: 1-10 minutes (Be sure to keep your legs *straight* but *not* locked during the entire movement.)
	Move #43	Floating Side Scissors: 1-10 minutes
Muscle Strengthening and Toning Exercises	Move #53	Outer/Inner Thigh Scissors
	Move #54	Forward and Back Leg Glide
	Move #57	Hip Side Press (version 1)
	Move #59	Supported Squats (Add these when you have minimized your knee pain.)
	Move #60	Calf Lifts
	Move #61	Toe Lifts
Final Cool-Down Stretches	Perform the same stretches recommended during Warm-Up, but hold the static stretch positions for 20 to 30 seconds.	

Intensifying Your Water Workout

T oo often people miss out on the benefits of regular exercise because, they say, "I don't have enough time." Aquatic Exercise
Association training specialist Julie See describes aqua power and
plyometric aerobic exercise as the perfect timesaving solution because
they combine aerobic conditioning (and fat burning), strength training,
muscle endurance, flexibility work, and a refreshing dip in the pool into
one concentrated workout.

Power and plyometrics are relatively new terms used to describe advanced fitness techniques. *Power* refers to "push-off" moves that use
gravity, your body weight, and the floor to build strength and aerobic
intensity. *Plyometrics* refers to "jump training" techniques that emphasize explosive leaping and bounding moves that can raise aerobic intensity and challenge your muscles.

Once you have attained basically good physical fitness, you can make
excellent use of your time and speed up your workout results with aqua
power and plyometrics. If you have built strong and flexible muscles,
particularly in the torso in order to protect your back from injury, the
Power Moves and Plyometric Moves described in this chapter can propel

you into advanced levels of fitness. Water allows you to increase intensity in a protective atmosphere unavailable on land. Water's bouyancy provides the perfect environment in which to perform these advanced fitness activities once limited to sport-specific training and body building. Aquatic buoyancy supports the body structure, so it reduces stress on the joints during challenging moves. Water's resistance, on the other hand, increases the toning and strengthening effects of power and plyometric techniques.

REACHING HIGHER LEVELS OF FITNESS

Power moves involve a variety of squatting exercises that make the large muscles of the buttocks and thighs work hard. The continuous action of large muscle groups like these activates the aerobic energy system, improving cardiovascular endurance and burning fat stores. Properly performed, water squats also tone the muscles of the legs and buttocks by forcing the lower body to work against the resistance of your body weight and water's viscosity. Aquatic buoyancy, meanwhile, takes the pressure off your joints.

Plyometrics are powerful, controlled impact jumps composed of explosive upward leaps. Plyometrics increase strength, endurance, coordination, reaction time, and aerobic and anaerobic capacity. Use of proper technique and preparation is essential for injury prevention.

ACCOMPLISHING MORE IN LESS TIME

What makes aqua power and plyometric aerobics particularly beneficial is that they allow fit individuals, even those who have recuperated from injury, to accomplish more conditioning in less time. Power and plyometric moves allow you to combine cardiorespiratory conditioning (aerobic exercise) with strength training and muscle toning through the use of exercises that elevate the heart rate into the aerobic working range while strengthening the muscles against water's resistance. So in one hour, you can accomplish twice the duration of aerobic exercise and toning activity possible in a regular format that calls for a separate toning section. *However, to prevent injury*, start by adding a few power and plyometric moves to your program and then gradually replace your regular water aerobic moves with advanced moves one by one.

POWERING YOUR WAY TO FITNESS

Alternate the Power Moves in this chapter with plyometric and regular aerobic moves for variety, and to maintain your aerobic target heart rate. As you improve your execution of Power Move exercises, you will be able to use them to maintain your target heart rate throughout your power and plyometric aerobics segment using a few plyometric or regular jogs, jumping jacks, or slides simply for transitions between exercises.

Power and plyometrics will contribute great variety and intensity to your workouts. Practice the basics and perform them with complete control before you add these mighty moves to your program.

Exercise Precautions

People with joint problems, hypertension, or heart disease should seek guidance from a qualified medical or fitness professional before performing aqua power or plyometrics. Power and plyometric exercises can be introduced comfortably and safely once you have developed a moderate level of strength, flexibility, and awareness of good body alignment.

Using Proper Power Technique

You will be more comfortable if you start your Power Moves in waist-deep water. Before entering the water, practice your stance in front of a mirror (stand sideways) and compare your body position with Figure 8.1. With practice you will be able to balance yourself so that you can "hover" over an imaginary chair situated a foot or two, or 30 to 60 centimeters behind you while using the following technique to protect your knees and spine. For squats, make sure your knees are over your heels, not your toes, your buttocks are pressed back as if you were about to sit in a chair, your back is *not* arched, your chest is lifted, and your

Figure 8.1   Correct body position for proper power technique.

abdominals and buttocks are held firmly to brace and protect your spine. Remember to breathe properly.

Power Move Guidelines

- Warm up and stretch all of the muscle groups beforehand to improve exercise efficiency and reduce risk of injury.
- Distribute your weight evenly around your body's center of gravity (usually somewhere near the navel) and maintain the braced neutral position at your pelvis to help maintain proper body alignment. Strong abdominal muscles are a must.
- If your main objective is overall toning and endurance, limit the amount of resistance (use little or no resistance equipment) and do a high number of repetitions. If you want to increase strength and develop more muscle shaping and definition, increase resistance and decrease repetitions.
- Always perform Power Moves slowly and with control, particularly when using resistance equipment.
- For good fitness results, squat to the depth that is comfortable (pain free) and within your complete control, but to no further than 90 degrees of flexion at the knees. Practice and perfect move #59, Supported Squats, from chapter 5 and move #79, Simple Squats, in the next section, before attempting to introduce Power Moves into your routine.
- To increase resistance with power moves: Add equipment such as webbed gloves or a kick board, plastic plate, or Frisbee held gently but firmly in both hands at waist height while you squat (Figure 8.2). Add resistance conservatively only after you have built a strong foundation and can perform the moves with complete control.

Figure 8.2   Equipment, used properly, increases resistance and builds strength and endurance.

Power Moves

Move #79: Simple Squats

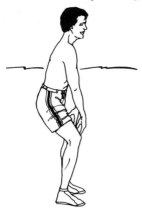

Starting Position: In waist-deep water, stand with your feet shoulder-width apart, knees pointing the same direction as your first and second toes.

Action:

1. Imagine that there is a chair approximately 12 inches behind you and push your buttocks back and down toward the chair. Squeeze your buttocks as you squat, pull your abdominals in firmly, and balance your weight evenly front-to-back and left-to-right.
2. Squeeze your buttocks and the backs of your thighs to press yourself back into a standing position.

Repeat 16 times.

Variation: Change the distance between your feet to work the muscles differently.

Move #80: Squat Press

Action: Repeat the action of Simple Squats.

1. Straighten your arms at your sides. As you squat, extend your arms out in front of you, scooping your palms toward the surface of the water. Keep your chest lifted.
2. As you rise, turn your hands around and press your palms down, returning your arms to your sides.

Repeat 8 to 16 times.

Move #81: Squat Knee Lift

Action:

1. Perform the Squat Press.
2. As you rise, add a right knee lift.
3. Squat again and as you rise, add a left knee lift.

Alternate right and left sequence for 8 to 16 repetitions.

Move #82: Squat Knee Curl

Action:

1. Perform the Squat Press.
2. As you rise, kick up your right heel toward your buttocks and draw your elbows back behind your waist.
3. Put your right foot down as you squat press again.
4. As you rise, kick up your left heel toward your buttocks.

Repeat the sequence 8 to 16 times.

Move #83: Squat Scissor Lift

Action:

1. Squat and bend both arms at the elbow, pressing your palms toward your chest.
2. As you press yourself into an upright position, lift your right leg out to the side. At the same time, straighten your arms and press them out to either side.
3. Bring your leg back in toward your body. At the same time, squat and bend both arms at the elbow, pressing your hands toward your chest.
4. Repeat, but press your left leg out to the side.

Repeat the sequence for eight repetitions.

Safety Tip: Maintain control by maintaining the braced neutral position. Keep your leg low if you have ever experienced any back pain.

Move #84: Squat Step

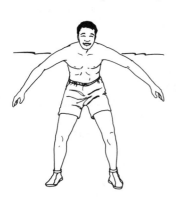

Action:

1. Squat and step out to the right at the same time. Press your arms out to the side as you step out.
2. Bring your left leg in to meet the right as you stand upright and bring your palms to your sides.

Repeat for two large steps or four small steps.

Change direction and repeat the sequence: Step out with your left leg and draw the right leg in to meet the left. Repeat for two large or four small steps.

LEAPING INTO FITNESS

Pushing your body upward through water elevates your heart rate and trains your muscles to gain "plyometric strength." Pushing off the pool bottom and leaping—sideways, forward, straight up, or into a tummy tuck—trains your muscles to marshal a great amount of force into one exertion. Repeating this exertion of force progressively overloads your muscles and cardiovascular system.

Using Proper Plyometric Technique

When starting out, raise yourself up onto your toes instead of leaping until you feel comfortable pushing off the bottom of the pool. This will help you develop control over your body alignment technique and reduce your risk of injury caused by improperly performed leaps.

Start in waist- to chest-deep water, depending on what is most comfortable for you. Hold your abdominal and buttocks muscles firmly when you leap to avoid arching your back and straining your spine as your feet leave the bottom of the pool. Always land with bent knees and, whenever possible, bring your heels all the way to the floor.

Plyometrics Guidelines

- Before you add plyometrics to your workout, be sure you have developed a good to excellent level of flexibility and strength. Strong abdominal muscles are particularly important.
- Warm up and stretch all the muscle groups beforehand to improve exercise efficiency and reduce risk of injury.
- Distribute your weight evenly around your body's center of gravity (usually somewhere near the navel).
- Land lightly, minimizing floor impact and contact time.
- Use the braced neutral position and keep the body in proper alignment. Keep your back straight, your chest lifted, and your ankles and knees in a bent (flexed) position, and land with your shoulders over your knees. When you elevate into a jump, be sure your abdominals and buttocks are pulled in firmly to brace your spine in neutral and avoid hyperextension (inward curve) at the lower back.

Plyometric Moves

Move #85: Peter Pan Side Leap

Starting position: Coil into a feet-together minisquat to prepare for a powerful push-off. (This position is shown in Figure 8.1.)

Action:

1. The basic move for a side leap is a step-apart side step. Imagine that you are leaping over a hurdle sideways, starting with your right leg. Press your palms out to either side.
2. Land softly and bring your left leg in to meet your right. Bring your palms down to your sides.

Repeat four times. Then repeat the sequence in the opposite direction, starting with the left leg. Land softly and bring the right leg in to meet your left.

Move #86: Hurdle Hop

Starting Position: Coil into a feet-together minisquat to prepare for a powerful push-off. Reach both arms out in front.

Action:

1. Lead with your right leg as you push off your left foot into a forward leap. At the same time, press both palms out to the side in a breast-stroke motion.
2. Land on your right foot and bring your left foot forward to meet your right.

Repeat four times, leading with the right leg. Turn around and repeat four times, leading with the left leg.

Move #87: The Dolphin Jump

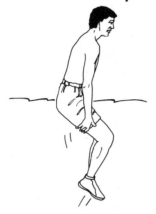

Starting Position: Start with feet shoulder-width apart. Coil into a mini-squat like in Move #84 to prepare for a powerful push-off.

Action:

1. As you push off the bottom of the pool, tuck your abdominals and bring your knees in toward your chest. As you jump, extend your arms out in front and press your palms in toward one another.
2. Land lightly with bent knees, bring your hands apart, and push off again.

Repeat 8 to 16 times.

Variations: Push your palms toward one another under your thighs. Or perform facing the pool wall or ladder, and hold on with both hands. Highly advanced version: Coil your body with your hands at shoulder height. As you push off, reach overhead, pushing toward the sky. As you land, bring your hands back to shoulder height. Keep a slight bend at your elbow to protect the joint, and maintain a firm hold on your abdominal and buttocks muscles in the braced neutral position.

Move #88: Plyometric Jack

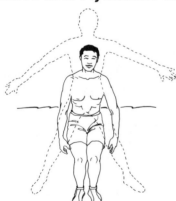

Starting Position: Coil into a feet-to-gether minisquat like you did for Move #84 to prepare for a powerful push-off.

Action:

1. Push off the bottom and jump up, drawing your knees up and coiling into the tummy tuck. Then bring your legs apart, pressing both hands to the sides. (Keep your hands under water.)
2. Land lightly with your feet wide apart, knees slightly bent, heels down.
3. Push off the bottom and jump up, coiling into the tummy tuck. Then bring your legs back in and knees up.
4. Touch down lightly with your feet just shoulder-width apart.

Repeat 8 to 16 times.

Move #89: Plyometric Ski

Starting Position: Begin with right foot in front, left in back, firmly bracing your spine in the neutral position between contracted abdominals and buttocks muscles. Reach forward with the left arm, back with the right.

Action:

1. Coil slightly, then push off the bottom and jump up. As you jump, draw your knees up, squeeze your torso into the tummy tuck, and switch legs and arms.
2. Land lightly with your left foot forward, right foot back; right arm forward, left arm back; knees slightly bent.

Repeat 8 to 16 times.

Move #90: Hip, Hop, Hooray!

Starting Position: Begin this highly advanced exercise with your feet shoulder-width apart, hands raised to shoulder height.

Action:

1. Coil slightly, pulling in your abdominals and buttocks, and push off the bottom of the pool, kicking your legs out to either side. At the same time, press your arms up overhead, just in front of your ears. Avoid locking your elbow joint as you straighten your arms.

2. Bring your feet together and land lightly with slightly bent knees in a minisquat, bringing your heels all the way down. At the same time, bring your elbows down toward the water's surface.

Variation: Stand in waist-deep water at the pool wall and perform the same exercise holding on to the edge of the pool, pushing with your arms as you jump up and bring your legs apart. Keep your legs pointing toward the bottom of the pool and your elbows slightly bent. This variation requires advanced upper body and torso strength.

Safety Tip: Limit the number of repetitions to avoid the lack of control that always accompanies fatigue.

Index

Page numbers in italics refer to figures and tables.

About the Author

MaryBeth Pappas Gaines has taught group exercise and water fitness programs since 1982. She is the Health Promotion and Fitness Administrator for Simmonds Precision, Inc., B.F. Goodrich, and is the founder of "Body In Motion," a corporate and community fitness company that specializes in aquatic exercise programs, and of American Health & Fitness, a training organization that teaches health and wellness information to fitness instructors, coaches, and worksite employees. MaryBeth also has been a personal fitness trainer since 1989. Her private practice serves clients with special concerns and specializes in corrective and adapted aquatic exercise and water workout recovery programs.

MaryBeth graduated from Rutgers University in 1979. She is certified as a personal fitness trainer by the National Academy of Sports Medicine and as a health and fitness instructor by the American College of Sports Medicine, the American Council on Exercise, the Aquatic Exercise Association, and the National Arthritis Foundation. In 1993, she was appointed to serve on the Vermont Governor's Council on Physical Fitness and Sports. In her free time, MaryBeth enjoys beachcombing, reading, and organic gardening.